Singing American English

Textbook of Diction for Singers

John T. Blizzard

Second Edition

Singing American English

Textbook of Diction for Singers

Singing American English

Textbook of Diction for Singers

John T. Blizzard

This book is dedicated to the late Dr. James C. McKinney,
dean of the School of Church Music at Southwestern Baptist Theological Seminary,
and all of my diction students, who teach me so much.

Wingate University
Wingate, North Carolina
© 2012

Acknowledgements

I would like to thank several people and institutions for their part in making this textbook a reality. I couldn't have done it without you, and I am grateful for you.

First, my thanks to my late parents. They taught me so much—especially with regard to language—giving me the encyclopedia to read as a child and Noam Chomsky's work to discuss as a pre-teen. I felt that I could ask them just about anything, and they would know the right answer. Of course, their typical response (which did me quite a lot of good, it turns out) was: "Look it up." Thanks, Mom and Dad!

Next, my thanks to Wingate University. The semester of sabbatic leave I enjoyed in the spring of 2011 gave me the luxury of time for study and writing which I would not otherwise have had with the busy schedule that comes with a life of teaching, ministry, and performance. The Wingate/DuPont Summer Research Grant I enjoyed with student Wesley Watts a decade ago was also a major impetus for the writing of this text.

A huge thank you to my great colleagues on the faculty of the Department of Music at Wingate University for their encouragement in this endeavor. Their extra efforts in taking up the slack during my sabbatical have been most appreciated. Thanks especially, Jessie Wright Martin and Melinda Lein!

Thanks also to my family for their patience and understanding during the many times this labor of love took me away from them, my deadline looming ever larger as the next semester approached. Thanks, Luci!

My sincere thanks to the church choirs I have learned so much from, especially the outstanding Choir of St. Stephen in Charlotte, North Carolina, where I am privileged to serve as minister of music. I'm not sure if I've mentioned it lately, choir, but diction is important. Thanks also to my tremendous associates, Julia Hubbard and Michael Lehtinen!

Thanks to the many diction professors and authors I have learned from in my own training. I continue to learn new things every year. Thanks also to diction professors Daune Mahy of Oberlin College, David Adams of the University of

x

Cincinnati College-Conservatory of Music, and Kathryn LaBouff of Juilliard and the Manhattan School of Music, who allowed me to observe their classes during my sabbatical study, and especially Professor François Loup of the University of Maryland for his marvelous insights into vowels and resonance.

Finally, thanks to the many students in the diction for singers classes I have taught over the years, as well as my own voice students. You have taught me so much, and I look forward to learning more.

Blessings to all of you.

Table of Contents

INTRODUCTION

I have long felt the need for a new text on singing American English, for soloists, choirs, teachers, and directors. There are many textbooks which I have used, but with which I have had disagreement at some point or other, either in content or approach, or both. Having taught diction for singers for many years, and having been a student and performer of it even longer, I now share with you my own approach to singing American English. This text is intentionally somewhat conversational in tone, and it sounds a great deal the way I speak in class; therefore, the pronouns "I" and "we" appear with some frequency. I hope that, rather than being a hindrance, this will be of benefit to you in the sense of having a guide alongside you on your personal journey—gaining the knowledge, experience, and interpretive artistry you will share with the world.

SINGING "STANDARD" AMERICAN ENGLISH

Several thoughts may come to mind when we encounter the labels "Standard American English" and "General American Pronunciation." Singers come from every part of the world, and they have a wide variety of accents in their speech, but the sounds they use on the recital hall and operatic stages can be remarkably different from their spoken sounds—much more uniform in production and accent—because there are patterns or means of production that work better than others in terms of ease of function and intelligibility.

A second aspect of the topic is that, overall, the resonance used in singing can be very different from that used in speech. We typically use much more resonance in our singing than in our speech, and we pay closer attention to articulation in our singing than in everyday speaking. Depending on the tempo and rhythmic values, we often sustain vowel sounds much longer in singing than in speaking, and with more oral space, resonance, and breath energy.

One more consideration is that American English is different from various forms of British English (BBC style, Received Pronunciation, etc., and even the hybrid "Mid-Atlantic" or "Cross-Atlantic" style often used in oratorio singing). This may be obvious to some people, but not everyone, as evidenced by current usage on the recital stage. I think the influence of certain textbooks and approaches to the singing of English have held sway far too long. To sing a contemporary American art song in the style of English speech used so wonderfully by actor William Powell in the film *Life with Father* (1947)—as beautiful as it is—can sound very affected. While there are occasions when a more British pronunciation may indeed be preferred, or the Mid-Atlantic style, it will be the intent of this text to focus on the Standard American

English style.

HEARING

There are even vast differences in the various ways we perceive language in our own hearing compared to others', as audiologists are able to demonstrate. Take my grandmother, for example. When my niece was born, she asked me, "What will they call her?" I replied, "Alix." She said, "Ah, Ellix, how pretty." I thought that perhaps she hadn't heard me clearly, so, later in the conversation, I mentioned Alix's name again: "Aaa-lix," I said. And yet again, she referred to "Little ELL-ix." I imagined the vowel ladder of IPA symbols in my mind, thinking, "Hmm, it seems her vowel system is skewed one symbol (counter-clockwise) to the left." In other words, she used too much tension in the forward arch of her tongue.

This stayed with me (obviously). She often referred to "Ellix" in phone conversations. Several years later, when my first grandson was born, another opportunity came my way: "What will he call you?" she asked. I thought, "Oh, man, I have just one chance to get this right—otherwise, she'll mispronounce it forever." (Yes, such was my trust in my grandmother's ear.) Slowly, carefully, even deliberately, I said, directly into the phone, "PAH-pah" (Papa). She replied, "Aww, 'Pă-pă' (with the short /ah/ sound, as in the word "hat")—how sweet." Slapping my forehead, I thought, "NOOOO!!!!! I had my one shot, and I blew it!" Of course, in hindsight, I realize that if I had guessed, "Now, let's see, if her vowel system is skewed counter-clockwise on the vowel ladder, then I should tell her that he's going to call me 'Paw-paw,' then who knows what would have happened? Would she have indeed skewed it to PAH-pah, or would she have repeated it back exactly as I had said it? By some miracle, would that part of her vowel ladder have been more accurate in her hearing and speaking? Or would she have dropped even further down that side of the ladder (clockwise) and gone, "POH-poh"? Aieee! Alas, the dye was now cast forever.

As long as we're on the subject, when is the last time you had your hearing checked—ever? It's difficult, if not impossible, to hear the finer differences among all of the sounds we'll study if you can't hear the full spectrum of sound.

GOALS

Distinguishing among various sounds—increasing your "sound set"

One goal of this text is for you to increase your ability to distinguish among various sounds, and to increase the number of those sounds, comparing and contrasting them, and being able to hear the differences. This concept has been called "expanding your sound set." Figuratively, your "ears" will then be growing. When confronted with two vowels in close proximity, some students will comment, "But they sound the same." My response is usually, "Right now, they do," because I hope that by the end of the course, they will hear differently--learning to tell more and more sounds apart. I tell students that my goal is to make them have "bigger ears--huge ears," so they can fit in all of the sounds we will study. As David Adams puts it: "Nevertheless, it is hoped that some of the fine points discussed will at least make the student more sensitive to various nuances of language. Taken together, such nuances comprise a potentially powerful expressive arsenal for the singer."[1]

Going hand-in-hand with developing a larger set of sounds that you are able to hear, develop the ability to perform that same ever-increasing number of sounds. Think of this as a three-way connection: ears, brain, and voice. You hear the sounds, your brain processes them and gives commands, and your voice performs them.

Clearly communicating and expressing, without calling attention to the diction itself

With all of the work you are to undertake on your journey, expanding your ears, increasing your sound set, and developing your ability to distinguish among sounds and to articulate them, keep in mind that the ultimate goal will not be for your diction to call attention to itself—unless that's the point of the song or aria—but, rather, for you to get out of the way of the words, so that the communication of the text to your listeners can be free and unhindered, easy to understand. It's interesting to hear compliments from audience members who seem surprised that they "understood every word." It's also a little sad that they aren't able to understand the words more often when listening to performers.

As an experiment, I had a class of students stand (one at a time) on our recital hall stage. They selected a passage from the Psalms to read to their class audience, and in their best, projected speech, would read the passage. I then called on someone else in the class, sitting in the audience, to tell the speaker and the rest of us what they had just heard the speaker read aloud. The student speaker was often disheartened at how poorly they had been understood, but the experiment really showed them just how much energy and careful attention are needed in learning how to communicate with ease. As Geoffrey Foreward puts it, "The words you sing have great beauty, with power to move emotions. But for this magic to happen, you must follow two unbreakable rules of communication: (1) You must be heard. (2) You must be understood."[2] Years ago, voice pedagogue D. Ralph Appelman observed:

When excellent diction is part of a singer's established technique,
the listener recognizes instantaneously the word that is directly related to

its familiar pronunciation within speech forms. Therefore, it is the singer's duty, throughout all migration in pitch changes, to preserve the integrity of the authentic phoneme [a distinctive unit of speech sound] and not to select a migration that will cause the phoneme to migrate in a direction that is unnatural and will not enhance the vocalic sound.[3]

Beautiful speech

Our goal in diction for singers classes isn't necessarily to improve a student's speech, but if the study of diction has that effect, that's great. Of course, some aspects of singing can be very different from speech. We typically use much more resonance in our singing than in our speech, and we pay closer attention to articulation in our singing than in everyday speaking.

But there should be wonderful trade-offs between great singing and great speech—that is, they should go hand in hand.[4] I'll never forget when my first grandson was a little boy. One day, as I was going on and on about something, he looked up at me quizzically and said, "Papa, you sing when you talk." I was taken aback, then thought for a moment, and said, "Thank you." What a nice compliment. Two things I tell my students are, "Sing from the depth of the abundance of the riches of your voice," and "Cultivate and develop beautiful speech." Why shouldn't it be pleasant to listen to you speak as well as sing?

Beautiful speech is something that's missing in a lot of American society today, and perhaps it always has been; when we hear a speaker with beautifully mellifluous tone, we take note of how very different they sound from the average person we encounter. Some pockets of American society even use a "vocal fry" in their speech, as if attempting to artificially lower their speaking voice, or to demonstrate (sometimes in an unintentionally comical way) their lack of concern for whatever the topic of conversation is. Finding the best pitch range for our voice can be an eye-opening (or "ear-opening") experience. Many Americans habitually speak in a pitch range which is not optimal for their voice—either too high or too low—causing either undue wear and tear on the mechanism, wasted energy in production, and even unintelligibility. Virgil Anderson commented:

> Individual voices differ markedly in the pitch to which they most easily and naturally respond, the natural pitch being determined by the essential structure of the voice mechanism itself, principally the length and weight of the vocal folds. As a matter of fact, within reasonable limits, the pitch of the individual voice is not the most important factor in

determining its excellence; many good speakers have voices that are naturally high, for example. The important consideration is that the pitch should be right for that particular voice.[5]

Anderson continues with helpful instructions for finding the optimal pitch level for your speaking voice.[6] Note that the term *pitch* is used here to describe an average range of notes, not a single frequency resulting in a droning monotone. (Imagine a lecture class done that way.)

Think about beautiful speech as you learn more about the relationship of diction to your voice.[6] That way, you won't go around speaking the way Kurt Adler must have heard people do, when he suggested that we keep our singing diction far away from our speaking, when he wrote: "One of the most widespread errors is that spoken and sung sounds are the same. Nothing is further from the truth. To sing the way you speak may be advisable for popular music, but it would make the voice sound brittle, harsh, and uneven in opera, song, and choral music."[7] One wonders how "brittle, harsh, and uneven" the speaking was of those he heard around him. James McKinney put it another way:

> There are obvious differences, of course, for speech and song do not sound alike, but these are differences in degree or extent of usage. Persons who are skilled at both speaking and singing can pass from one to the other with apparent ease; this is a necessary skill in opera and musical comedy, where the medium shifts back and forth between singing and spoken dialogue with little or no pause. Regardless of the skill of the singer-actor, it is an easy matter to ascertain which medium is being used, for there are significant differences.[8]

Learning the International Phonetic Alphabet

You'll get to learn more about the International Phonetic Alphabet (IPA) in Chapter 2, but for now, keep mastery of IPA in mind as one of your goals. It is such a helpful tool for singers in that we get to think in more specific terms about each sound we make when singing. Think of the difficulties we have anyway in spelling American English: combine the /gh/ in "tough," with the /o/ in "women," add in the /ti/ in "action," and you get: "ghoti": gh-o-ti, (say it slowly): /f...ih...sh/—that's it—"fish." Working with a system of sound symbols can be very helpful to us in focusing on the correct way to pronounce, articulate, and express a song text.

Again, because this is a text for singing Standard American English, we will not deal so much with other styles, such as Mid-Atlantic, the many Southern types, and various British forms. Readers are encouraged to refer to resources which include those styles, such as Kathryn LaBouff's *Singing and Communicating in English*[9]

As you learn IPA, many of the symbols will come easily to you, but there may be some which present more difficulty. While it is easy to get frustrated at first, keep pressing on toward success. The connection between your eyes/ears, brain, and voice can continue improving, like playing a sport or any other skill. Remember, you're not only gaining knowledge of pronunciation rules, but you are adding a skill. And being able to hear the finer points of difference among a wider and wider variety of sounds is a wonderful skill to achieve, worthy of your time and effort. As I tell my diction students, "I want your ears to grow."

THE TONGUE
Correct positions, without the "invisible spoon"

There are some aspects of free articulators we can experience with the aid of a mirror. This is worthy of some attention at the outset. When you sing an [i] (long ee) vowel or an [ɪ] (/ih/) or [ɛ] (/eh/), does the tip of your tongue stay at the back of your lower front teeth? Try this exercise, using a mirror at first, place the tip of your tongue against the back of your lower front teeth. Next, brush the tip of your tongue against the back of your lower front teeth, back and forth. Now sing an [i] vowel and do the same brushing motion. Try it again without looking in the mirror. Try to feel the connection between the tongue and the teeth even while you're singing, making sure that excess tension in the tongue isn't pulling the tip away from the back of the lower front teeth on vowels from /ah/ to /ee/.

The "back of the front teeth" position for the tip of the tongue doesn't work for all vowels though. As we will see in the coming chapter on vowels, about half of them should be sung differently. Actually, to attempt to sing every vowel sound with the tip of the tip of the tongue at the back of the lower front teeth can create a lot of unnecessary tension. For example, moving from /ah/ to /ooh/, the tip of the tongue pulls away from the back of the lower front teeth as it arches up in the back of the mouth.

If the tip of your tongue is indeed in the right place, how about the general shape of the tongue? If you're singing an /ee/ vowel, does it seem like there's an invisible spoon depressing the front of the tongue? That kind of tension can actually make an /ee/ vowel sound like an /ih/. Do a few exercises to loosen up your tongue—

such as /lah...ee... lah...ee/ and /loo...ee...loo...ee/—to find a more relaxed-looking tongue arch in which [i] really sounds like /ee/, and not like /ih/. You can try exercises which use both the front and back of the tongue, like /ga la, ga la/ or /la gi, la gi/, etc.

My "Mom story"

Finding and developing control of the tongue, and the persistence in practice that it can take, reminds me of my mother. A wonderful person, she taught all subjects and all grades of students who were, for whatever reason, unable to go to school, mostly one-on-one, as a "homebound teacher" for much of her career as an educator.

Well, one semester she had a student in beginning Spanish. My brother and I had studied the language, so she called on us for help. I said, "Okay, Mom, let's try this word. Say, 'rojo.'" She looked perplexed and said, "Say that again?" I said, "rrrrrrrro-jo," emphasizing a trilled or rolled /r/. She replied, "Udder, udder, udder, udder...row-hoe." Again, I repeated the word, this time really making the rolled /r/ and the pure /o/ vowel easily heard. She knitted her brow and tried even harder: "Udder, udder, udder, udder...row-hoe." Thwacking myself on the forehead, I said, "Hey, Mom, I gotta go." (I have no idea how the rest of the semester went with the unsuspecting student.)

Fast-forward fourteen years, and I was sitting in her hospital room. She'd been fighting ovarian cancer for several months, and I had come to see her for what turned out to be the last time. We enjoyed tying up loose ends and expressing our love and appreciation for each other. As we discussed my teaching, we came to the subject of diction for singers; I remembered her failed attempts at a rolled /r/ from years earlier and said, "You never did learn how to roll an /r/, did you?" "What do you mean?" she replied, pushing herself up in her chair with her brow furrowed. Sitting up straight and tall, and taking a good breath, she said in a suddenly very strong voice: "Rrrrrrojo!" Wow! I couldn't believe it. My face lit up. How had she done it? She said with a self-satisfied grin, "I've been practicing."

I was amazed, as anyone would be. She had gone from zero ability to roll an /r/ to a beautiful, native-sounding trill. Like a baby, she had tried and failed, tried and failed, and kept on trying and failing. But then the day came when she started to hear and feel the beginnings of the /r/, and she kept going, kept practicing. It makes me realize that, unless there's some physical/medical reason holding a person back, they could learn how to speak any language on earth with enough time and persistence. Of course, it's easier when we're babies—hey, no bills to pay, no projects to get completed. At the top of the baby's list of priorities is sleeping, eating, pooping, and...learning how to talk. The moral of the story is: no matter how difficult a sound seems, and no matter how long it takes to conquer it, keep trying a little every day, and eventually you'll get there.

APPROACH OF THIS TEXT

Overall, this text may be used as a reference, for personal study, or in a classroom setting. I hope that it will be of benefit, as well as have an influence, not only in my own classes, but beyond, to the singing public at large.

The approach of this textbook will be for you to:

see it,

hear it,

sing it

You will see the symbol for a sound, hear it sung, and then sing it yourself. You can also then practice using the symbol in transcribing phrases and singing them.
Enjoy!

[ði ˌɪn tɚ ˈnæ ʃə nəɫ fə ˈnɛ tɪk ˈæɫ fə ˌbɛt]

Diction and Musical Artistry | Chapter 1

Welcome to the study of diction—especially as it applies to American English, and even more particularly as it applies to singing it. Broadly, diction can be thought of as an umbrella term, encompassing at least four different elements:

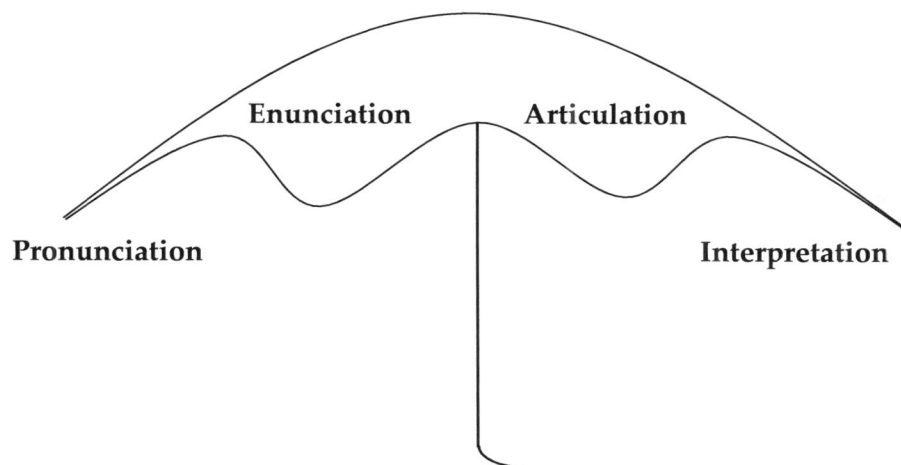

```
        Enunciation      Articulation

Pronunciation                        Interpretation
```

Pronunciation

The first element, pronunciation, is simply the way a word is pronounced in a given language. Traveling around the United States, you can hear words spoken in a variety of ways. However, listening to professional recitalists and oratorio and opera singers, we find greater uniformity of pronunciation (albeit, with some differences among genres). It is as if those singers are wanting to do away with their speech regionalisms for awhile in order to allow the maximum number of audience members around the country to understand their words. We could call this pronunciation more of a **Standard American English** (also called General American Standard, among many other labels). We hear this also in the speech of national news broadcasters.[10] They may have grown up in the deep South, or New England, or Texas, but you'd hardly realize it to hear them speak professionally. As we listen to them, we're able to understand all or almost all of the words. The goal of their speech has been accomplished, and the connection, the communication, is made.

Enunciation

The second element, enunciation, is defined in various ways—even synonymously with other terms—and involves clearly communicating the text in a way that makes it easier for the audience to understand. When a person is mumbling, we may want to tell them to enunciate their words. Enunciation is intentional in terms of energy, projection, and conveying meaning and expression through the use of the articulators, which brings us to the third element: articulation.

Articulation

The third element, articulation, is the use of the articulators in the production of vowels and consonants. The articulators include:

the tongue

the gum ridge behind the upper front teeth (called the *alveolar ridge*)

the teeth

the jaw (also called the *mandible*)

the hard palate

the soft palate (also called the *vēlum*)

the lips

and the glottis (the space between the vocal folds where we produce the sound /h/)

Keep in mind that not all of the articulators are actively engaged in producing every language sound. In Chapter 3, you'll see that we can even classify consonant sounds according to which of the articulators are involved.

Interpretation

A fourth element, interpretation, means how the use of diction is involved in your expression of the text, conveying what the mood and emotion are, and how your character uses language in the song or aria. We can express so many different things with changes in the diction we use; we're like painters with large palettes in a portrait studio. The poet has given us the foundational substance, and the composer has further enlightened us as to the meaning of that foundation. In the minds of some, we take it one more step— showing what it is all about, leaving the audience then to decide what it truly means to them. In our endeavor to interpret what the music means, what the text says, and what the poet and composer had in mind, we have to be careful, as Pierre Bernac reminded us:

> When a composer sets a literary text to music, he has his personal conception of the feeling expressed in the text, and it is this feeling that he attempts to express in his music. It may happen that the interpreter has quite a different view of this text, and thus finds himself torn between the two feelings he is required to express: that of the poet and that of the musician. Once again it is the musical feeling that must be given priority, since it is the musician who gives his personal interpretation of the poetic text, and it is essentially *this* interpretation that the performer is required to bring alive. He must therefore attempt to bring his own conception of the poem in line with the composer's, without of course losing any of his own personality.[11]

Communication

All of these elements of diction add up to the communication of an idea, a mood, a poem or other text, an atmosphere of emotion and meaning. And we get to do it through music. This is artistry. We are performers on a stage, inviting our audience on a journey with us, transporting them to another time and place, and causing them to feel something, or even to think differently about themselves and the world.

The singer should remember that there ought to be a congruency between their stage portrayal and the diction. In other words, there should be an agreement between what we're singing and the visual elements of our performance. Diction is a tool in our arsenal, our repertoire of expressive means on the stage. It is therefore worthy of our utmost attention and care, and the effort that it takes to develop ourselves in the realm of linguistics. It goes beyond our ability to hear the differences among sounds in various languages—even our own—and even beyond our ability to reproduce these sounds in our own singing. It is musical artistry, and it is simply wonderful.

4

The International Phonetic Alphabet | Chapter 2

The International Phonetic Alphabet (IPA)

The International Phonetic Alphabet, or IPA, has been a useful tool for singers and teachers of singing since its beginnings in 1888. It owes much to the "Visible Speech" work (1864) of Alexander Melville Bell, father of the inventor of the telephone, but he was not the first person to give thought to trying to represent sounds in symbolic form. Benjamin Franklin's diaries from the late 18th century show some of his thinking in attempting to write the sounds of his name in various ways. Many of today's textbooks, training manuals for singers, and reference books, including dictionaries and other works, use IPA or variants thereof to symbolize how particular words sound. We call the IPA symbols for a word its *transcription*, and the correct way to write it in its language the word's *orthographic spelling*.

Thinking in terms of sound symbols is of immense benefit to the singer. Having to decide what sound is wanted causes us to think more definitely about the vowel sounds we sing. As a result, our audience's ability to understand the words we are communicating can be vastly improved. It is a discipline to transcribe our songs and arias, but well worth the effort. IPA also gives a student and his or her teacher a common "language" to communicate what sounds are desired in a given phrase. If modification is needed, the teacher can ask for the sound by the symbol name, and the student can remember how that sound feels in order to produce it correctly. The same is true for choral ensembles. In transcribing texts into IPA, we use brackets to denote the symbols of distinct sounds:

peas [piz]   soup [sup]

The system of sound symbols that is IPA also includes diacritics (small marks) in its extended set which make changes in the sound symbols, denoting whether they should be more produced more forward, back, bright, dark, with a breath release, etc. Diacritics are also used to alter the sounds of letters in many languages—such as the tilde as in the word "señor" (Spanish) or the cedilla (*cédille*) in the name "Fran-çois" (French), the umlaut in "schön" (German), the grave accent in "è" (Italian), etc.

But even using the extended set of symbols in the International

Phonetic Alphabet, there are limits to exactly how much descriptive detail we can give with regard to specific sounds. The finest graphic representation can only give us an approximation at best. As Dr. Martin Néron lamented: "Indeed, IPA alone provides only a limited indication of the sounds of a specific language."[12]

Pay close attention to writing the symbols correctly, in order to avoid confusion with other sound symbols. Alternatively, if you're writing a paper and need to use IPA, try one of the excellent online resources such as http://ipa.typeit.org/.[13] This textbook uses the characters from that website (which come in the Charis SIL font), altered to the Lucida Sans Unicode font. The rest of the text is in Palatino Linotype.

CONSONANT SYMBOLS

b d f g h j k l ɫ m n ŋ p ɹ s ʃ t θ ð v w z ʒ tʃ dʒ

b	**b**oy		ɹ	**r**ed	
d	**d**og		s	**s**ee	
f	**f**og		ʃ	**sh**e	"esh"
g	**guy**		t	**t**ea	
h	**h**ay		θ	**th**ick	"theta"
j	**you**	(glide)	ð	**th**en	"ethe," "crossed /d/"
k	**k**ite		v	e**v**er	
l	**l**ight		w	**w**ise	(glide)
ɫ	ba**ll**	(backward /l/)	z	**z**oo	
m	**m**y		ʒ	vi**s**ion	"ezh," "cursive /z/"
n	**n**ot		tʃ	**ch**ur**ch**	unvoiced affricative
ŋ	si**ng**	"eng"	dʒ	**j**u**dge**	voiced affricative
p	**p**en				

8

Consonants | Chapter 3

Consonants in the International Phonetic Alphabet

One great thing about learning the International Phonetic Alphabet symbols for the consonants is that, as an English speaker, you know several of them (15) already. They are:

b, d, f, g, h, k, l, m, n, p, s, t, v, w, z

To these we will add several more, both individually and in combination with others, filling out all of the sounds used in singing Standard American English. There will be a couple of ways to do the /l/, but as examples, let's use those fifteen sounds with a few basic vowel symbols to get you started(/ee/, /ih/, and /ah/—[i ɪ ɑ]). The /ee/ sound (as in "beet") is represented in IPA by the little /i/, so we call it "little i." The /ih/ sound (as in "fit") is symbolized by the "big i" symbol, and the /ah/ sound (as in "father") by the symbol [ɑ], called "dark a." (This is in contrast to [a], the "bright a," which we'll learn more about later.)

/ee/   as in "see"   [si]

/ih/   as in "bit"   [bɪt]

/ah/   as in "stop"   [stɑp]

Here are more examples of IPA transcription, using consonant symbols you already know, as well as the three vowels mentioned:

beat	[bit]	dim	[dɪm]
feel	[fil]	knock	[nɑk]
feet	[fit]	fit	[fɪt]
fib	[fɪb]	fob	[fɑb]
hop	[hɑp]	geese	[gis]
peas	[piz]	kick	[kɪk]

Try not to get confused in going back and forth between a word and its transcription. The IPA for "feet" looks a lot like the next word, "fit." Remember, when it's in brackets, we have to think in terms of <u>sound symbols</u>. What are the sounds we're singing?

Note the difference in the transcription of the letter /s/ in the words "geese" and "peas." In the word, "peas," the final /s/ is "voiced"—that is, the vocal folds are vibrating—so it takes the sound of /z/. We call the /s/ in the word "sit" an "unvoiced /s/." To use an unvoiced /s/ at the end of "peas" would change the word to "peace." More about that later. In the last word, "kick," we use the symbol [k] for both the initial and the final consonant sounds.

Now you try it! Transcribe the following words into IPA:

sit	[	]	steep	[	]
sip	[	]	please	[	]
tick	[	]	tock	[	]
sock	[	]	top	[	]
clips	[	]	keys	[	]

Note: In the last line, "clips" uses the symbol [k] for the initial sound, rather than a /c/.

Consonants and vowels

Consonants can be contrasted to vowels in several ways:

- They are less open than vowels, restricting the flow of sound in some way.

- They define syllable margins, as opposed to carrying the tone to the audience.

- They need more energy in order to be projected to the audience.

- They involve more of a noise element in their production.

- They may be "unvoiced" or "voiced" (called *fortis* and *lenis* by linguists and phoneticians[14], involving more or less strength in their production). This is unlike vowels, which are all voiced (unless we're using a stage whisper).

Categories of consonants

Consonants can also be categorized in different ways. We can group them according to where they are produced (that is, how they are made or articulated):

resonated in the nose	nasal: /m/, /n/, and /ng
both lips	bi-labial: /b, p, m, w/
lip and teeth	labio-dental: /v, f/
tongue and teeth	lingua-dental: /th/ (voiced and unvoiced)
tongue and gum ridge	lingua-alveolar: /d, t, n, l/
tongue and soft palate	lingua-velar: /g, k, ng/
the space between the vocal folds	glottal: /h/

We can also group consonants according to whether or not we actually sing them (that is, *phonate*, or produce sound in the larynx), rather than their simply being noise elements which remain "unsung." These often occur in pairs, called "cognates." To determine if a consonant is voiced or unvoiced, simply place your hand on your throat. Do you feel vibration on your hand? If so, it's voiced; if not, it's unvoiced. Try it with /t/ and /d/, feeling the difference between these cognates. See the chart of cognates further below in this chapter.

Another way we categorize consonants is whether or not they can be sustained. This separates the plosives (quickly exploded consonants like /p, b, t, d, k, and g/) from the continuants (consonants which can be continued), which include the *fricatives*, for example /f/ and /v/, and *sibilants*, for example, /s/ and /z/, etc.

Further differences in consonants are made regarding whether or not they are linked into other sounds, for example, the /r/ in "ever" is different at the end of a phrase than when it is in the middle, as in "ever and always." There will be more about this in the discussion of the sounds of /r/.

ADDITIONAL CONSONANT SYMBOLS

The letter /c/

The letter /c/ can have several sounds in American English. It can be symbolized by a hard /k/, as in "case." It can take a soft /s/ sound, as in "face." And it can combine with other letters, such as /h/ to form the sound beginning and ending the word "church."

The letter /d/

The letter combination /ed/ can take the sound of /d/, or the unvoiced sound of a /t/, in final position following an unvoiced consonant. When /ed/ comes after a voiced consonant, the /d/ is voiced. For example, listen to the difference between the ending of "bagged" (/d/) and "backed" (/t/).

Forward and backward /l/

There are a couple of ways to represent the /l/ sound in IPA. We use the more forward, bright, clear one (just like in several other languages) for initial and medial (middle of a word) consonants, and even some finals, especially if they link into oncoming vowels. The backward /l/ is symbolized by [ɫ] in IPA. The word "ball" ends with a backward /l/ . Sing the word "ball" with both a forward and a backward /l/, and hear the difference. Using a forward /l/ at the end of "ball" would sound like American English sung with a foreign accent, as if the singer were a non-native speaker of the language. However, if it appeared in the phrase "ball and glove," we would use the forward /l/. Sing both of these phrases slowly, hearing and feeling the difference between the forward and backward /l/:

Throw me the ba<u>ll</u>! [ɫ]   (backward /l/)

Ba<u>ll</u> and bat   [l]   (forward /l/)

Likewise, using the backward /l/ at the beginning of a word can often take longer to articulate and is heard less clearly. Compare singing the word "land," beginning with a forward /l/ and a backward /l/.

The letter /q/

The letter /q/ is symbolized by [k], just like the hard /c/. In English words, it will typically combine with /u/ to form [kw], as in the word "quiz."

Practice the /q/ by transcribing these words into IPA:

quick   [   ]   queasy   [   ]

Now transcribe these words from IPA into their orthographic spelling. (Think of practice in this way as getting to know IPA inside-out, or backwards and forwards):

[mɪ ˈstik] _____   [kwɪk] _____

Note that in IPA, the accented syllable in these examples is denoted by a vertical stress mark above and to the left of the syllable, with a space between the syllables. The choices to be made in representing the sounds of syllables in written form can be difficult as well as limited. Syllabification differences among the way words appear in a score, or poetically on a page, the way they are represented in IPA, and the way they are sung can be quite numerous, as Leslie De'Ath's describes:

> Apart from individual letter symbols, words can be dissected into their segmental components in several ways. A word can be considered to be a string of discrete phonemes within a language, like pearls on a strand, or as a complex flow of articulative motions occurring simultaneously. The former is the traditional approach that is axiomatic to IPA transcription methods. The latter comes closer to reality, but lacks a clear nomenclature matrix or graph that does full justice to the complexity of human utterance, while remaining visually simple.[15]

Hard and soft /r/

The sound of the American hard /r/ is represented in the International Phonetic Alphabet by the symbol [ɹ], which is simply the /r/ symbol turned upside-down. (Flipping the symbol back the upright way actually represents a different sound in IPA: the trilled /r/ in Italian, Spanish, etc.) In the sound of the American hard /r/, we *retroflex* the tongue—bend it up and pointing backward toward the hard palate. Let's add another vowel symbol to your IPA repertoire, the /ooh/ vowel (called "little u": [u]), and see some hard /r/ words transcribed:

red   [ɹɛd]   rude   [ɹud]

rod   [ɹɑd]   read   [ɹid]

Note the use of another IPA symbol, the "epsilon," for the sound of "eh." It looks like a backwards "3."

Now you try a few with four of the vowel symbols you now know:

bread   [   ]   brewed   [   ]

drop   [   ]   breed   [   ]

Not all of the words in Standard American English that are spelled with the letter /r/ use this hard consonant sound. Some use the soft /r/, which is actually a vowel sound, either accented, unaccented, as in the word "learner" ['lɝ nɚ]. In other words, here, neither syllable uses the hard /r/ consonant sound, but instead, the /r/ is a vowel sound, as in "urge," "turn," "summer," "number," etc. Our singing of Standard American English is called *rhotic*-accented, because we use elements of /r/ before consonants and at word endings, unlike those dialects and accents which are *non-rhotic*. For example, singing the word "card" as if it were /kahd/ would be <u>non</u>-rhotic. More on these vowel sounds later.

One eye-opener for students of diction for singers is the change the /r/ makes in some word connections, a kind of *liaison*, as Madeleine Marshall borrowed the term from French diction.[16] Singing a word such as "forever" at the end of a sentence takes one kind of /r/ sound, a soft one—actually a vowel sound. But linking the word into an oncoming vowel means that a harder sound of /r/ has to be inserted—an actual consonant. In the phrase "forever and ever," the word "forever" has two of the hard /r/ sounds—one in the middle of the word, and the other linking into the word "and." The end of the last word, "ever," has the softer sound of the /r/. Learn to recognize the differences in the way these two sound and feel.

Interestingly, some choral directors and voice teachers tell students to avoid the American hard /r/ altogether, no matter where it occurs in a word, as if it were some terrible thing. Others have students flip the sound of /r/

like the Italian version, symbolized by [ɾ] in IPA. This leaves singers sounding as if they either have an indolent tongue like a cartoon character, ("wed, wed, wose") or that they're not from the United States. To quote Dorothy Uris: "But to American ears, a superimposed trill or flip impresses as affected if not outlandish. It would seem to be a patriotic duty to rescue the American-English /r/, a fine sound when well made."[17]

Here is an example[18] of the way treatment of the poor /r/ is taught, presented in a humorous, rhythmic (but, in this writer's opinion, misguided) approach. Unfortunately, many choral directors and voice teachers would concur with this view. My responses are italicized beneath each line:

An "R" before a consonant: take it out!
(So "heart" would then be sung as "hot"?)

An "R" between two vowels: flip it about!
(Perhaps if the children were oratorio singers using Mid-Atlantic pronunciation, but otherwise, could they just retroflex the /r/ similar to the way they would speak it, albeit even more beautifully?)

An "R" before a vowel: let it be, let it be.
(Paul McCartney's words were never put to such good use! What if we just "let it be" in the other two instances above also?)

or you'll find yourself up a "tee," not up a "tree!"
(Right, so back to the "heart"/"hot" thing mentioned above....)

Pity the poor, maligned /r/! Obviously, we wouldn't want to use the American hard /r/ at phrase ends like "foreverrrrr." But let's learn how to sing it well, use it when needed, and bring that sound back into the singing repertoire.

The letter /s/

Like the letter /c/, the /s/ has two basic sounds and can be combined as well. It can be sung unvoiced as /s/ in the word "case," or it can be voiced as a /z/ in the word "rose." It can even combine with /h/ as /sh/ to make the [ʃ] sound, called "esh," as in "fresh." Be careful not to put the tip of the tongue forward all the way to the upper front teeth, causing a lisping sound to occur. Feel where the blade of the tongue (behind the tip) lightly presses up against the alveolar ridge. The tip of the tongue should feel as if it's touching nothing but air.

If you've never taken a look at your voice in a spectrogram, find one and try it out. It's interesting to see that so-called "pitchless" consonants (unvoiced) actually <u>do</u> have pitch—albeit a very high one—over an octave above the right end of the piano. But as high as an /s/ may be, some singers habitually produce that consonant even higher than they should. Experiment with sustaining a hiss for a minute, making the /s/ sound go as high and as low as you can. Did you realize you can make that many "pitches" on that consonant? Work with your voice teacher to make sure your placement of the tongue is exactly where it should be for the /s/.

DIGRAPHS

A digraph can be thought of as its syllabic roots imply: double-writing. These are two-letter combinations which form sounds other than what the letters would imply on their own, such as the /ph/ sounding as /f/, etc. Vowel combinations can also be considered digraphs, like the /ea/ in the word "each" and "peace," or the /ie/ in "niece" or "piece." To help you learn more of the consonant symbols used in IPA, here are several of the more common digraphs used in American English.

The /ng/ sound, as in "ring"

The symbol for the /ng/, known as "eng," looks like a combination of the /n/ and the /g/: [ŋ].

ring [ɹɪŋ]   sing [sɪŋ]   bring [bɹɪŋ]

Note: all of the /ing/ spellings in American English are transcribed in IPA with [ɪŋ].

The ng sound can also occur in spellings which use only the /n/, rather than /ng/, as in:

rink [ɹɪŋk]   sink [sɪŋk]   brink [bɹɪŋk]

The /ng/ spellings in English can make for some peculiar difficulties in singing American English. Some even use the hard /g/ following them, as in "finger." Note that this is not the case in words like "singer" and "ringer."

When singing words with /ng/, be careful of a few things:

1. not to change a final /ng/ to /n/, unless that's your intention when using a dialect.

Sing: bringing ['bɹɪŋ ɪŋ]   rather than ['bɹɪŋ ɪn] ("bring in")

2. not to change a medial or final /ing/ to another sound.

not ['bɹɪŋ iŋ]   ("bring eeng")

not ['bɹɪŋ in]   ("bring een")

and not ['bɹiŋ in]   ("breeng een")

but ['bɹɪŋ ɪŋ]   ("bringing")

It is especially good to pay attention to when there's another oncoming vowel, such as in the phrase "bringing on."

Sing: bringing ['bɹɪŋ ɪŋ ɔn]   rather than ['bɹɪŋ in ɔn]

When sung incorrectly, this actually sounds like "bringy non," which doesn't make much sense. For monosyllabic words like "king," sing [kɪŋ], not [kiŋ]. Here, think of the vowel sound in the word "kick" rather than "key".

3. and not to insert a hard /g/ or /k/ after a medial or final /ng/.

This may involve intentional re-learning for some singers of American English, depending on the regionalisms in their speech. Coordinated positioning of the tongue and soft palate for the release of the /ng/ will make for a beautiful [ŋ] without an intrusive /k/ or /g/, especially in final position, when we time it with the end of the sung tone.

Sing: bring [bɹɪŋ]   rather than   [bɹɪŋk] or ['bɹɪŋg]
Sing: song [sɔŋ]   rather than [sɔŋk] or [sɔŋg]

Be careful not to insert a /k/ sound when there isn't one written. For instance, in the word "length," be careful not to pronounce it as "lengkth." The same is true for the word "strength." It takes some careful listening as well as re-training the coordination of your articulators to get rid of a habit like that. One technique to practice singing this cleanly is to close the jaw for the /ng/ sound, then move on to the /th/. (We would usually allow the jaw to remain dropped following whatever the sound preceding the /ng/ required.) Also, you might try hanging on to the /ng/ longer than normal.

The same is true in avoiding a /k/ or /g/ release at the end of a word, such as "song" becoming "songk" or "song-guh," "long" being sung as "longk" or "long-guh," etc. Practice the smooth release of the /ng/ sound without an unnecessary plosive at the end.

An /n/ followed by a /g/ or a /k/ sound often changes to an /ng/, as in "bank." But in longer words, this depends on how the word is syllabified. For instance, in the word "ongoing," the /n/ and the /g/ are in two different syllables (on-go-ing), so the /n/ isn't affected by the /g/. But in the word "singer" (sing-er), the /n/ and the /g/ are in the same syllable, combining to form the digraph /ng/. This is also true of words with other vowels preceding the /ng/ sound, such as "anchor," "lengthen," "anger," "longer," and "hunger."

Note: In the last three words, the /ng/ sound is present as well as the hard /g/ which follows:

anger   [ˈæŋ ɡɚ]

longer   [ˈlɔŋ ɡɚ]

hunger   [ˈhʌŋ ɡɚ]

(All of the vowel symbols used above will be discussed later in detail.)

Now transcribe these words into IPA using the symbols you've learned:

sing   [   ]   sink   [   ]

kingly [   ]   linked   [   ]

pink   [   ]   pinging [   ]

Remember, in the word "linked," the final /ed/ doesn't sound as a /d/, but as a /t/.

Try going from IPA back into the orthographic spelling with these words:

[mɪŋk] _____   [ˈstɪŋ kɪŋ] _____

The /sh/ and /zh/ sounds

The /sh/ is represented in IPA by the symbol [ʃ], pronounced "esh," which looks like an elongated /s/:

ship   [ʃɪp]   dish [dɪʃ]

shoes [ʃuz]   she's [ʃiz]

Note that both capital letters and punctuation (including apostrophes) are not accounted for in the International Phonetic Alphabet. Remember, we're just representing sounds in symbolic form within the brackets.

The voiced counterpart (cognate) of the /sh/ sound is the /zh/ sound, called "ezh," and represented in IPA by the symbol [ʒ], as in:

rouge [ɹuʒ]   vision [ˈvɪ ʒən]

The vowel symbol in the second syllable of the word "vision" is called a "schwa" (pronounced [ʃwɑ], from the Hebrew word transliterated as "shva"). It is used for so many unstressed vowels, it is the most frequently heard sound in American English. We'll learn more about this vowel later.

Now you try a few. Transcribe the following words into IPA:

luge   [   ]   wish   [   ]

she'd [   ]   wash   [   ]

Transcribe these words from IPA into their orthographic spelling:

[paʃ] _____   [ɪ 'lu ʒən] _____

[liʃ] _____   [ʃut] _____

The /th/ sounds: voiced and unvoiced

The /th/ can be voiced or unvoiced, so we use two different IPA symbols to represent the difference. The voiced one is the "crossed d," [ð], called "eth" (pronounced [ɛð]. The unvoiced version is called "theta," like the letter from the Greek alphabet: [θ]. Here are a few examples of each:

Unvoiced:

think [θɪŋk]   thing [θɪŋ]

thick [θɪk]   thin [θɪn]

Voiced:

this [ðɪs]   these [ðiz]

then [ðɛn]   them [ðɛm]

Notice the differences between the word "breath" (a noun) and "breathe" (a verb):

breath [bɹɛθ]   breathe [bɹið]

Now you try a few. Transcribe the following words into IPA:

thief   [   ]   myth   [   ]

seethe [   ]   wreath [   ]

Gothic [   ]   soothing [   ]

Note: In the last two words, remember to put the vertical accent mark up and to the left of the stressed syllable.

Sing and write these transcribed words in their orthographic spelling:

[ɹuθ] _____   [tɹuθ] _____

[θɪk] _____   [θim] _____

[buθ] _____   ['ti ðɪŋ] _____

Affricatives

Affricatives are combinations of plosive and continuant consonants. These include the sounds in "<u>ch</u>ur<u>ch</u>" [tʃ] (unvoiced) and "<u>j</u>u<u>dge</u>" [dʒ] (voiced). If it's difficult to imagine the plosive sound as truly existing before the continuant in these words, try one without putting the plosive in there, for instance "itch" [ɪtʃ] would become [ɪʃ], rhyming with "fish." Feel the tongue move to the alveolar ridge behind the upper front teeth first. The plosive has to be in there to make it work. The same is true for its voiced counterpart, the affricative [dʒ]. Feel the /d/ position before the /zh/ sound? The /d/ is a plosive, and the /zh/ is a continuant. Imagine if the /d/ were not in there. The word "fudge" would sound like fake French: "fuh-zh." (It might sound funny, but it would probably still taste great.)

Here are some examples of affricatives, both voiced and unvoiced.

each [itʃ]   ridge [ɹɪdʒ]

reach [ɹitʃ]   fridge [fɹɪdʒ]

Now you try a few. Transcribe the following words into IPA:

beach [   ]   rich   [   ]

dodge [   ]   Jewish [   ]

Note: In the last word, a /w/ isn't needed in the IPA, as if the second syllable were "wish." Also, remember the accent mark for the stressed syllable.

Be careful not to skip over the position of the plosive, going instead straight to the continuant. For instance:

sing "actual"   as   ['æk tʃu əɬ]   not   ['æk ʃu əɬ]

Getting the blade of the tongue (behind the tip) up to the alveolar ridge (behind the upper front teeth) while the /k/ is taking place is helpful. That way, we not only <u>do</u> pronounce the /t/ sound in the affricative, but we also avoid putting the puff of a silent /ih/ vowel between the /k/ and /tsh/.

Sing and write these transcribed words in their orthographic spelling:

[dʒus]   _____   ['fi dʒi]   _____

[hadʒ padʒ] _____   [tʃɪn]   _____

['tʃu zi]   _____   [pɪtʃt]   _____

Remember, a final /ed/ spelling after an unvoiced consonant is sounded as a /t/.

COGNATES

We have mentioned several pairs of voiced and unvoiced consonants. Let's take a different look at them in list form. Sing each pair, hearing and feeling the differences:

Voiced	Unvoiced
b	p
d	t
v	f
g	k
ð	θ
z	s
ʒ	ʃ
dʒ	tʃ

It should be noted here also that there are a few consonants which don't have a cognate as far as this text is concerned: /h/, /l/, /m/, /n/, /ɹ/ (the American hard /r/), and the /w/. Some phonetics texts add more pairs, such as /w/ and /hw/, but we'll learn more about why these are not a part of such a list later in the chapter on glides. Also, the term *cognates* is used differently in phonetics than it is elsewhere in the realm of linguistics, such as in the many words brought into American English from other languages, for example *sombrero* and *beret*. Spanish and French, both descended from Latin, are called *cognate languages*.

CONSONANT ENERGY

The amount of energy we use in the articulation of consonants is dependent on several factors:

- **the acoustics of the space**

An auditorium with favorable acoustics requires less work on the part of the singer, in terms of the energy involved.

- **the relative dynamics of the phrase**

The consonants will typically not be as loud as the vowels surrounding them. This said, as we sing more softly, we have to keep in mind the threshold of hearing on the part of the audience. Therefore, softer singing may lessen the relative difference dynamically between vowels and the consonants surrounding them. We will see more on this in the section below on Diction and Volume.

- **the accompaniment medium**

Singing over a full orchestra can take more energy in terms of vowels and consonants, especially if there is a great amount of energy present in that part of the sound spectrum.

- **and the consonant's place within a word or phrase**

The amount of consonant energy can be thought of as being in this order of position (from the most to the least):

initial (at the beginning of the word)

final (at the end of the word)

medial (in the middle of the word)

The last category can also include final consonants which are linked into oncoming vowels, as in "I'd_always." Here, legato phrasing dictates that we link the /d/ softly onto the oncoming vowel. Some schools of thought say that all initial vowels should be given some type of a glottal attack, but it can become so intrusive as to chop up an otherwise beautiful phrase. It is amazing to hear how (unfortunately) proficient some singers are at using the technique of separation. Try singing this line:

"As‿ever‿I'd‿always‿imagined‿an‿azure‿umbrella..."

Do you connect the final consonants to the oncoming vowels, or do you separate them with light glottal attacks? Go for the smooth connection. It's really so much more beautiful—and easier on your audience's ears. They'll still understand you—they won't even hear the word "doll" between "I'd" and "always." Why? Because there won't be the energy of an initial consonant in the link. Remember? Initial consonants need the most energy. Think about it—that's how we speak.

We have to be careful with the amount of energy a linked consonant receives. Remember, it's a linked final, and not a full initial consonant. Pay attention to how much energy and time are given to the /n/ in the following phrases. Note the differences between singing:

in Asheville [ɪn   ˈæʃ vɪl]

and   in Nashville [ɪn: ˈnæʃ vɪl]

In singing the first phrase, the link between the final consonant of /in/ and the initial vowel of /Ashe/ means that the /n/ could be represented in the IPA as being in the second of the three syllables. But because it is a linked final consonant, and not an initial consonant, it gets less energy. In the second phrase, the same sound ends the first syllable and begins the second syllable, so we go into it sooner and sustain it longer, giving it extra energy.

DICTION AND VOLUME
Threshold of hearing, consonants and vowels/volume relationship

Remember that it's easier to sing louder on vowels than consonants because vowels obstruct the flow of sound so much less. While we are singing at a louder dynamic level, it's easy to keep consonants above the threshold of hearing for the audience, but it's more difficult to get the consonants to match the volume of the vowels. When we sing more softly, the vowels may be above the hearing threshold, but we have to be careful that the consonants don't drop below, depending on the acoustics of the room. That could make for a lot of difficulty in comprehension for the audience. In soft singing, the relationship of the dynamic level between consonants and vowels therefore needs to be much closer than when singing louder.

How we hear vs. How we're heard

Our perception of own volume and tone while singing is distorted compared to the way the audience hears us. We've all had the experience of hearing our voice for the first time on a recording, and thinking, "That doesn't sound like me," or "That sounds so different—is that really me?" What we think of as our voice is a combination of the sound conducted through our heads on its way to our ears, in addition to the sound coming to us from outside our heads. But our audience can only hear the part that's outside our heads. It makes sense then that, while we can use the sound in our heads as a kind of sensory guide, the sound we're really trying to improve is that which is outside our heads—the one the audience hears.

A danger here is that if we close off our vowels, and the resulting sound in our heads seems louder, we perceive that our voices are somehow bigger or richer also. But the audience—again, outside our heads—may perceive our sound as somewhat smaller, less full and rich. We have to remember that our sound is not to be hoarded in a selfish way, but rather to be directed outward—shared with our audience. Instead of closing off vowels, if we open them up, they may seem smaller inside our own heads, but actually louder to the audience; depending on the acoustics of the room, there can then actually be much more sound surrounding us, reflected by the walls and coming back to our ears.

DICTION AND RHYTHM

The length of a given vowel in a phrase depends on the oncoming consonant or consonant cluster, based on the syllabification, because we have to allow time to get through a group of consonant sounds. Where the next vowel opens is the determinant of the rhythm for the note to follow. That is, where the next vowel is sung is where the rhythm of the next note is. We sing the consonant preceding a vowel slightly ahead of the beat, so that the vowel can open right on the beat. Accompanists listen for this as well, knowing where the tempo the singer wants, based on where the vowels open. In the example below, the arrows represent where the beats might occur within a meter:

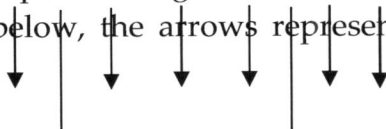

my   fa - ther was   go - ing

As we see here, the feeling of the beat in the rhythm and meter of a measure is helped by opening to the vowel at that point, rather than waiting to sing the initial consonant—voiced or unvoiced—and then opening to the vowel. Doing it the other way can actually give the feeling of slowing down the tempo, as if the singer were slightly dragging behind the beat. The same is true for choirs also.

Some advocate that unvoiced consonants (/p/, /t/, /k/, etc.) come before the beat, and that some voiced consonants (/l/, /m/, /n/, etc.) come <u>on</u> the beat.[19] But such is not actually the case when the consonant is linked into an oncoming vowel. Both voiced and unvoiced consonants should be sung slightly ahead of the beat, opening to the vowel on the beat or part of a beat as dictated by the rhythm. This is especially crucial in choral singing as well. But final non-linked consonants should come right on the next beat or part of a beat as notated. Keep in mind that it was the practice among 20th-century British composers to use a tied note to show where the end of a pitch was to come, rather than the tied note actually meaning to sustain the pitch for additional time. This can be seen also in the works of non-British composers influenced by that practice.

AMERICAN ENGLISH CHARACTERISTICS
Legato links, syllabic stress, parts of speech

In her textbook *To Sing in English*, Dorothy Uris labeled one of the main characteristics of sung American English "linkage-legato" (or "legato linkage").[20] She called another important characteristic "sense stress."[21] Briefly, this means that not every word in the language should receive the same amount of importance, or vocal weight, and that not every syllable should receive the same amount of stress. Thus, usually an article or a conjunction is not as important as an active verb or a descriptive adjective. Another way to think of syllabic stress is to "put the right em-<u>PHA</u>-sis on the correct syl-<u>LA</u>-ble.

Syllabic consonants, or "consovowels"

Occasionally, depending on the tempo and rhythm of a song or aria, and the style of articulation used, a syllable may not actually be sung with a vowel sound in it, even though it might be spelled with one. In that case, a consonant is taking the place of the vowel. That doesn't necessarily go against some definitions of the word "syllable," because, rather than having a <u>vowel</u> as its center, it has to have an area of greater <u>sonority</u> (usually the vowel), and possibly surrounded by whatever area(s) of lesser sonority—the consonant(s).

Take the word "him," for example. The /h/ is followed by the sustaining vowel /ih/, and the syllable ends with the /m/. But what about a word like "didn't"? It has two syllables, but in its contracted form, it doesn't have a vowel in the second one. So, what takes the place of the vowel sound? It's the /n/, which is a continuant, and here acting as a *syllabic consonant* or *consovowel*. Note: Plosives aren't used in this way, because they aren't sustained.

To signify the /n/ being used as a consovowel, a dot is placed under the consonant symbol in the IPA. Thus, the transcription could look like: [ˈdɪd n̩t]. We could even put the second /d/ in the next syllable, [ˈdɪ dn̩t], depending on the tempo, rhythm, etc. If the word "didn't" were to be sung on whole notes at a slow tempo, fortissimo, we would probably opt for a schwa in the second syllable in order to make it heard, like: [ˈdɪ dənt]. But if you're singing to an audience in a smaller hall, at a fast tempo, and the word "didn't" appears in the text, you might have time to open for the schwa, so a syllabic consonant would help greatly. Other examples of the syllabic consonant, or consovowel, include:

buttons	[ˈbʌt n̩z]	as opposed to	[ˈbʌ tənz]
little	[ˈlɪt ɫ̩]	as opposed to	[ˈlɪ təɫ]

Note: The word "buttons" includes the schwa symbols we will learn—both accented and unaccented. In an art song at a really fast tempo, the word "little" might even be heard as having a /d/ in the middle, rather than as a /t/. Both the /n/ in "buttons" and the final /l/ in "little"—in this case the backward /l/—are continuants. This feature of our language is similar to spoken German: the word "lieben" being shortened to [ˈli bn̩], and "haben" to [ˈha bn̩] (or even [ˈli bm̩] and [ˈha bm̩]).

The /d/ in the middle of the word "didn't" and the /t/ in "little" and "buttons" are articulated differently at a fast tempo than they normally would be as medial consonants at a slow or moderate tempo. There's a sense of stopping or even imploding (rather than exploding) them before quickly moving on to the continuant acting as a syllabic consonant. Try speaking the word "didn't" in slow motion, and feel the soft palate release after the /d/ to allow the sound into the nose for the /n/.

If you were to sustain the word "little" on whole notes at a slow tempo, another way to shape a vowel in the second syllable would be with an [ʊ]—the vowel sound in the word "could." Try it on a medium-high pitch for a few seconds. "Little" could be sung somewhere between [ˈlɪ təɫ] and [ˈlɪ tʊɫ]. As we'll see later in the chapter on vowels, these "tinged vowel" mixtures, or half-way points between vowels can be helpful in shading just the right vowel sound with the proper amount of syllabic stress. All of this is to help us make beautiful tones and to communicate with our audience. The relationship between those two concepts also depends greatly on the style of singing.

Consonant Blends, Pre-loading, and Transitions

Unlike digraphs, which are two consonant letters forming one sound, those combinations of consonants in which each letter is still heard are called "blends." For instance, the word "blend" even has a blend at the beginning—/bl/, and again at the end—/nd/. Each consonant is still heard in the blend, but no other sounds should be inserted. As examples of what this type of incorrect insertion can sound like, the words "praise" and "bread" are sometimes heard sung as "puh-raise," and "buh-red." In order to counteract this tendency, we can think in terms of "pre-loading" the next consonant on or within the preceding one. It's actually easy to do, especially with these examples, which involve pre-loading a lingual (tongue) consonant inside a bi-labial (both lips) one. To sing "praise" and "bread" correctly, we prepare the tongue by retroflexing it (bending it up and back) within the bilabial beginning consonant. That way, there is no schwa heard between the two consonants, and the move from one consonant to the other is sung much more smoothly.

Singers usually find fewer problems in singing other consonant combinations, even when they occur in a word or phrase other than in the initial position. Typical faults occur in words such as the examples below (shown with IPA transcriptions):

Sing "hosts" as   [hoʊsts]   not "host"   [hoʊst]

                                        and not "hōs"   [hoʊs]

Sing "facts" as   [fækts]   not "fax"   [fæks]

                                        and not "faxed"   [fækst]

Sing "texts" as   [tɛksts]   not "text"   [tɛkst]

                                        and not "Tex"   [tɛks]

The first example, "hosts," requires tongue control to go from the /s/ to the /t/ and back again. A part of that control is timing. If the word "hosts" appears at the end of a phrase, such as in, "O Lord of ho<u>sts</u>," we use the first /s/ as the preparation (before the beat), and the /ts/ as the release (on the beat.) Try singing that phrase on a sustained pitch in a 3/4 meter:

O   Lo- - - - - - - - rd of   hō-ō-s-ts

In the last measure, the /ts/ comes right on the third beat, rather than the /s/ which follows the /o/. It's as if the /s/ following the /o/ is almost on a half-beat (the "and" of beat two). It takes us too long to articulate /sts/ to count it as being all on one beat.

The word "facts" requires a great deal of tongue movement, all the way from the back of the mouth to the front: a lingua-velar unvoiced plosive (/k/) going to a lingua-alveolar unvoiced plosive (/t/). Again, go for precision (often speedy precision) in your articulation. For "facts," to check yourself, try putting a vowel between the /k/ and the /ts/ release, like făk-(ih)-ts. Now minimize the amount of /ih/ sound between them. Then take the vowel out completely. You can even practice going /k-ts/, /k-ts/, /k-ts/ several times.

For "texts," we think of the /ks/ sound as the preparation, and the /ts/ as the release, like /teh . . . ks-ts/. Thinking of the /ks/ as coming <u>before</u> whatever beat the release of the word is found on is very helpful. It gives us the time necessary to perform the articulation. Some singers want to hang onto the vowel too long, not allowing enough time to complete all of the consonant sounds needed. Practice that articulation move: /ks-ts/, ks-ts/, /ks-ts/. Gaining control of our articulators is similar to an artist learning brush techniques in applying paint to canvas. It's part of our artistic toolbox, and however long it takes us to gain mastery, that's the time we must invest.

When transitioning from a voiced continuant to another consonant in the next syllable—called a *merge*—(whether voiced or unvoiced), be careful not to insert an unvoiced plosive in-between them. For example:

constant	['kɑn stənt]	rather than	['kɑnt stənt]
infant	['ɪn fənt]	rather than	['ɪnt fənt]
Samson	['sæm sən]	rather than	['sæmp sən]
crimson	['kɹɪm zən]	rather than	['kɹɪmp zən]
		and not	['kɹɪmp sən]

Usually, if the plosive intrudes at all, it will be only stopped—especially with the throat (a glottal stop)—and not fully exploded.

It's interesting to see how less likely we are to insert a plosive when the oncoming consonant begins a stressed syllable as in:

inside   [ɪn 'saɪd] or ['ɪn saɪd]   instill [ɪn 'stɪl]

In such cases, we're not nearly as tempted to insert a /t/, no matter if the oncoming consonant is voiced or unvoiced. When the merge involves two nasal consonants, for example in the word "hymnal," simply sustain the nasalized /m/ all the way to the nasalized /n/, without releasing the articulators in-between. The audience shouldn't hear an /uh/, an /ih/, or any other sub-vowel between the /m/ and the /n/.

DICTION AND TIMBRE

The timbre (tone color) of our vowels is highly dependent on how we shape them. Many singers are capable of singing a wide variety of vowel colors, from very bright to very dark. Artistic and aesthetic judgment are a part of the process in determining how bright or dark to go, as well as how we want to present ourselves in terms of characterization, expression, and projection. Work with your teacher and listen to recordings of yourself to find out what the best color is for each word and each phrase in a song or aria.

There should be a congruency between the expression you're trying for, and the timbre of the voice. As you'll be reminded later in this text, because the positions on the vowel triangle you'll learn are not fixed—that is, our tongues, lips, and jaw don't "click" into position—there are many variables, and we have many choices to make in terms of vowel color.

Oral and Nasal Resonance

As listed earlier, there are three nasal consonants used in singing Standard American English: /m/, /n/, and /ng/. Nasality in singing vowels is a somewhat controversial subject. Some teachers adhere to the school of thought which says that no nasality is ever needed or even allowed when singing vowels. Others, particularly teachers of tenors, feel that a slight drop of the soft palate creates a beneficial lengthening of the vocal tract, making higher notes easier, and that any nasality heard in the tone is all a part of a tenor's "ring" in the timbre of the high notes. Consult with your voice teacher to see if any nasality you are experiencing is detrimental, or beneficial, to your singing. Also, listen to recordings of the tenors Fritz Wunderlich and Mario Lanza to hear nasality used in beautiful ways.

One quick method to determine if you are using nasal resonance is to sing while pinching your nostrils closed, as if you had a clothes pin on your nose. If the sound changes when you close and then release your nose, then you are most likely using some nasal resonance, because the sound isn't utilizing exclusively oral resonance.

Substitution

Of course, if you don't want to use nasal resonance when singing a vowel, there are ways to train yourself to avoid it. For instance, when the vowel precedes one of the three nasal consonants, the temptation is to drop the soft palate early for the nasal consonant as we might do habitually when speaking, making the vowel preceding it a nasal one, especially when the vowel is an open sound, such as [a] or [ɔ]—/ah/ or /aw/. In the examples below, the nasalized version of the vowels (with the soft palate down and forward) is represented in IPA by a *tilde* over the vowel, like the /n/ in the Spanish word /señor/.

Sing: lawn   [lɔn]   rather than   [lɔ̃n]

Sing: bomb [bɑm]   rather than   [bɑ̃m]

A particularly effective method to correct this is called "substitution." In this technique, we practice by changing the nasal consonant to a closely approximate unvoiced plosive sound (approximate in terms of articulatory position). For example, in the word "home," if the /m/ is causing you to sing with a nasal tone on the long /o/ vowel, as you would in singing a French word like "nom" ([nõ]), try substituting a /p/ for the /m/ ("hope," instead of "home") several times. Subconsciously, we tend to keep the soft palate in a more closed position when approaching the /p/. Now try singing it. Sing "hope," emphasizing the oral resonance of the long /o/. Finally, sing "home," but imagine that you're going to sing "hope," and at the last moment before going to the /p/, change it to an /m/. This technique has been successful in solving some nasality issues for many singers.

DICTION AND GENRES OF SINGING

The amount of attention we give to diction in singing depends on the style or genre we're performing. An operatic role will typically demand more tone (volume) than words. It would be incredibly difficult, if not impossible, to produce consonants at the same level as the loud vowels sung on the operatic stage. Singing in a Broadway show will usually demand more attention to the words than to the tone (with varying degrees of this, depending on which sub-genre). Wearing or using a microphone can allow all sorts of possibilities for nuance and keeping consonants about as loud as vowels.[22] And art songs in recital come somewhere between these two, in which we give attention to beauty and fullness of tone as well as clarity of text. One way to think of oratorio singing is that it's "art song on steroids" — that is, all of the tone and all of the words, and all of that projected dramatically over an orchestra right there on stage.

Here's a graphic way to represent these genres and the tone/word relationship used in singing them.

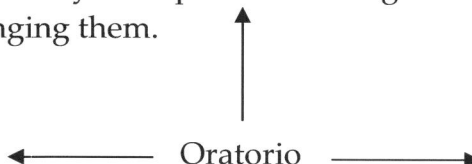

← —— Oratorio —— →

The Hellwag Triangle | Chapter 4

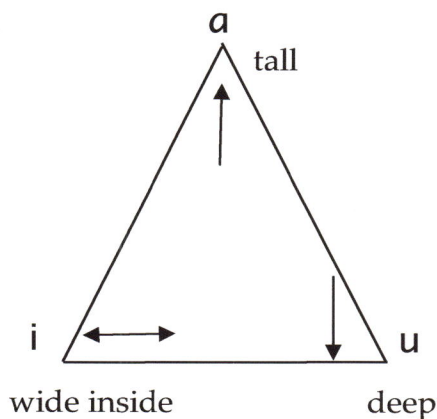

a
tall

i ←→   ↓ u

wide inside   deep

Vowel direction

In learning the relative positions of vowels in the International Phonetic Alphabet and the resonance demands involved in classical singing, we can use a vowel chart or diagram that you will see several times in this book. This vowel ladder, or triangle, devised by C. F. Hellwag in 1781, is of immense help to a singer, because knowledge of where vowels feel as if they need to "go" makes resonating them so much easier. It is as if we are "getting out of the way" of the vowel, making the right kind of shape, and with the ideal amount of room for it to blossom and project to the audience. Of course, in terms of physical science, we know that sound vibrations simply seek out the next space available, but it's the shaping of that space that makes all the difference.

In reality, this short chapter could be the most important one in this entire book, in terms of having an effect on your singing! Read it carefully, think about it, memorize it, and practice it to make it a natural, automatic, habitual part of your singing.

It is amazing how intuitive Hellwag was in terms of the physics of singing. His main conclusions—coming before the invention of the laryngoscope, X-rays, the electroglottograph, etc.—have been found to be correct—some within the last few decades.

The Hellwag triangle is really where pedagogy and diction meet—in the resonance involved in singing, and in the ways that it affects vowel sounds. Hellwag felt that the three corners of the triangle were the purest directional sense of the vowels:

/ah/   having the greatest need for vertical space in the mouth

/ooh/   the deepest (or furthest back)

/ee/   the widest inside

(Note that the "width" of the /ee/ is not a wide, "smiley" position on the outside, because <u>all</u> vowels can be thought of has having a vertical oval posture.)

Of course, there are more than just those three vowels in singing American English. What about the other vowels? They can be thought of as combinations of those directions. That is, an /ih/ vowel is very much like the /ee/ in terms of inner width, but with a little more vertical space toward the /ah/. The /ay/ and /eh/ are about halfway between the width of /ee/ and the height of /ah/. And the short /ǎ/ sound, as in "hat," has almost as much vertical space as /ah/, with a little of the "wide inside" quality of /ee/.

On the other side of the triangle, the short /u/ sound (as in "put") has much of the depth of pure /ooh/, but with a little more of the height, or vertical space, of /ah/. The long /o/ vowel is about midway between deep /ooh/ and tall /ah/. And the open /o/ sound, or /aw/, has much of the space of /ah/, but with some of the depth of /ooh/.

Feeling these directions when singing vowels can be incredibly freeing. When we get out of the way, singing is so much easier. Experiment for yourself. This concept could truly be the biggest breakthrough in singing you've ever experienced—a key to unlocking the fullness of your sound. (Your friends might not believe you when you tell them you learned about it in a book about diction.)

Anticipatory space

Another concept to keep in mind—as we make the appropriate tall/ deep/wide-inside direction and space for each vowel according to Hellwag's triangle—is what I call "anticipatory space," or even "anticipatory variable space." This is the idea that as we connect one sound to another, we can anticipate the direction and space for the oncoming sound. Why wait until you're already there and it's too late? Prepare each sound and shape slightly ahead of time, and you'll find it much easier to create beautiful, legato phrases.

As an example, on the words "He always, " according to the Hellwag triangle, the movement from the /ee/ vowel to the next one, /aw/, would be from "wide inside" to "tall, and a little deep." That's a lot of movement, as well as quite a change in vowel resonance "direction." In order to increase the legato in the phrase, we can borrow the position of the /aw/, and allow the initial vowel to feel not only "wide inside," as it should, but also "tall, and little deep," anticipating the position of the /aw/.

Try it yourself. Sing "He always" on a pitch in the middle of your range. As you sing the /ee/, anticipate the position of the oncoming /aw/ vowel. Can you hear and feel the differences between the two vowels? Do you hear how much easier it is to connect to the oncoming /aw/? Another way to think of this is that a given vowel sound that we're sustaining doesn't exist in isolation. When you go onstage to sing, you're going to connect sounds to other sounds. This is a way to make that action a lot easier and more beautiful.

As another example, and involving a different directional change, sing the phrase "You aim." In moving from the /ooh/ vowel (deep, according to the Hellwag triangle) to the long /ā/ (somewhat wide inside, but not quite as much as the /ee/ we saw earlier), again we see a lot of movement of the articulators. In moving from the depth of the /ooh/, we widen inside to prepare for the oncoming vowel and find that the legato connection is made.

Anticipatory space is important even when there is an intervening consonant or two (or more) involved. In singing the phrase "angels pass," if the word "angels" is on a low note, and the word "pass" is on a high note, for example, change the amount of room in your mouth (by dropping the jaw) as you make the initial /p/ of "pass." Then, when you open your mouth for the vowel, you already have the amount of oral space needed.

When large pitch changes occur in a score, again anticipatory variable space can be of great help. We normally wouldn't use a lot of space, say, medium-low in our voices, but adding the space ahead of time can make the leap a great deal easier. The resonance space needed for the high note is already there, and the vowel can flow freely, without a sense of having to push it through a smaller opening.

VOWEL SYMBOLS

ɑ	father, box, top, mod, Tom, pond
ɑɚ	are, car, star, bar, mar, par, csar
aɪ	file, I'd, eye, fly, smile, time, my
aɪɚ	fire, ire, mire, tire, choir, shire
aʊ	house, plow, crowd, how, mouse
aʊɚ	our, hour, tow'r
æ	tap, mad, sack, plaid, plaque
æə	yeah!
ɛ	let, bet, net, fête, debt, get, jet
ɛɚ	air, fair, mare, pair, rare, their, there, they're
eɪ	bay, hay, Jay, lay, paid, ray
ɪ	bit, hit, fit, lit, mitt, knit
ɪɚ	ear, here, rear, leer, near, pier, peer
i	see, be, key, Lee, tea, flea
ɔ	bought, caught, flaw, on, fall
ɔɚ	or, oar, horse, course, warm, door, pore
ɔɪ	boy, coy, ploy, toy, Roy, soil
oʊ	owe, row, hoe, bow, toe, shown
ʊ	put, book, full, pull, should, could
ʊɚ	your, you're, poor, sure, lure
u	boo, flew, gnu, shoe, to, too, two

Vowels	Chapter 5

i
ɪ
e
ɛ
æ
a
ɚ ə ɝ ʌ
(ɒ) ɑ
ɔ
o
ʊ
u

openness."

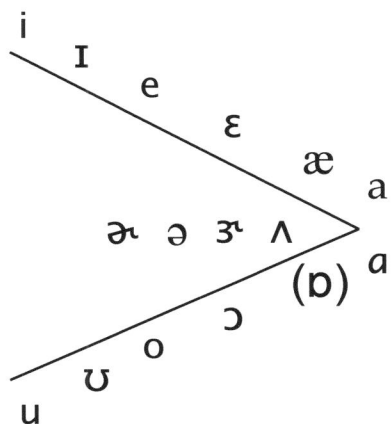

"All Vowels Are Open"

Although we learn closed and open positions for various vowels in the singing diction for various languages, essentially "All vowels are open." That is, they have an unrestricted quality of projection and resonance to them. To add to that short concept, we could add, "They just have open and closed positions within that

Vowels are sometimes placed into categories such as lip vowels (on the bottom side of the chart above) tongue vowels (along the top side of the chart), and central, or neutral, vowels (in the middle). But this can lead us to misunderstanding, since, in diction/articulation terms, the tongue is the primary determinant of <u>all</u> vowels—or, more exactly, the amount of space between the surface of your tongue (front/middle/back) and the roof of your mouth. In the realm of voice pedagogy, we would say that, based on the shape of the vocal tract (which includes the mouth), the *formants* are the primary determinant.[23] These are bands of resonant frequencies which contain more energy than other areas in our spectrum of sound. Regarding "vowel postures," the late Richard Miller wrote:

Vowels are continuants, capable of maintaining a specific vocal tract configuration and sustaining phonation. In singing, such a configuration of the vocal tract may extend through an entire expiratory phase of the breath cycle, if so desired. Unless vowels are improperly produced, no friction noises intrude during the sound. The characteristic sound quality of the vowel depends on the vowel formants, which have fixed values for each particular shape of the vocal tract.[24]

The lips are indeed normally more involved in the vowels along the bottom side of the chart above. Vowels are also categorized as being either "front" or "back," according to where the arch of the tongue is. But, again, if as a singer you prefer a brighter or darker tone, it might not help to think of a dark tone as being "frontal" or a bright tone as being "back."

As we have contrasted consonants to vowels previously, we can remember the following concepts relative to vowels:

- All vowels are open (with a feeling of unrestricted flow of sound).

- Vowels make up the majority of almost all syllables, carrying the tone to the audience.

- Vowels can be thought of in terms of "direction," according to the Hellwag triangle (seen in the previous chapter).

In the middle of the triangle are four central or neutral vowels. Interestingly, these vowels can, like colors of paint, be mixed with other vowels on the upper and lower sides of the triangle to create hybrid sounds. These are quite useful in singing, and they give us many more options in terms of modifying vowel sounds, coloring the tone in various ways, and best of all, increasing our ease of communication with the audience. We'll see more on this later.

Shadow vowels

Many choral singers and soloists alike are familiar with the concept of shadow vowels. These are brief vocal utterances following final voiced consonants, such as a soft /ih/ following the /v/ in the word "love." (The /ih/ is usually recommended over the schwa (/uh/, [ə]) as the shadow vowel in order to maintain intonation more easily). In transcribing song texts, we generally do not even take these into account in the IPA, but they can help final voiced consonants to be heard by the audience.

Of course, shadow vowels can be overdone. If the shadow vowel is too strong, or easily heard, it could be thought of as "coming out into the light," rather than remaining in the shadows—pun intended. A word such as "love," with too much shadow vowel, could be mis-heard as "lover" by an audience. This is even worse when a schwa is used, instead of /ih/, for instance, in singing "one" as "one-uh."

Shadow vowels should be sung judiciously. There is definitely an art to it. Final voiced continuants (non-plosives) can actually be sung with no release sound at all—simply take the breath away from the tone. Listen to professional singers, record yourself, and ask your teacher to help you determine how much shadow vowel to use. (You don't want to be the one person in choir cutting off a note with a shadow vowel when nobody else does.)

Vowel integrity

When singing a vowel before a final consonant, be careful not to allow the vowel to migrate away from its true sound. Be aware of the position of your articulators while sustaining the vowel in order to help maintain the integrity of the vowel sound.

Sing: him [hɪm]

and not [hɪ   əm]   or [hi   əm]

and not [hɪ   əɬm]   or [hi   əɬm]

Note: The above style of vowel sustaining can actually be utilized to good effect when singing in dialect. See LaBouff's *Singing and Communicating in English* for ideas in various non-standard dialects.[25]

In looking at the vowel chart both a couple of pages back, as well as through the rest of this chapter, you may wonder, "Why are the big /i/ and the /u/ so close to the smaller /i/ and /u/ symbols?" This goes counter to the way vowels were taught for years in diction classrooms, but it is in keeping with the official chart of the International Phonetic Association. Compare the vowel diagram in a text such as Moriarty's *Diction*, long considered the standard for the teaching of diction for singers, with the official chart of IPA, especially with respect to the placement of the closed /e/ and /o/.[26]

[i] and [ɪ]	/ee/ and /ih/

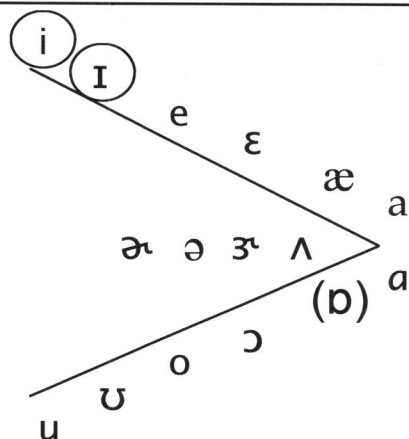

On the Hellwag triangle, the [i] vowel is the one he called "wide inside," that is, the throat needs to widen out sideways. This should not, however, be seen as being wide on the outside, as in a broad smile. Going that way reduces the richness in the resonance in the sound, giving it a brighter (sometimes more harsh), more shallow quality. Singing wide on the inside keeps the vowel in line with the rest of the sounds within a beautiful phrase, rather than sticking out suddenly. The [i] and [ɪ] vowels (called "little /i/" and "big /i/" for convenience) have various spellings in American English, such as in the words:

seem [sim]   receive [ɹɪ ˈsiv]   team [tim]   busy [ˈbɪ zi]

Note two things in the transcriptions of the words "receive" and "busy": the symbol for "ih" is used in the unstressed syllable in "receive." It can be thought of as relaxing the [i] vowel and finding that the [ɪ] works quite well. It is in a pre-stress syllable, and doesn't need as much intensity as the [i] does. But post-stress, as in "busy," the /y/ keeps the [i] sound in American English, rather than going for a more British-sounding "bih-zih," in spite of what some American English diction texts have advocated for years.

To make these two vowels, the tip of the tongue should be at the back of the lower front teeth, or at the back of the gum ridge below them. The body of the tongue arches up and forward, reducing the amount of space between the surface of the tongue and the roof of the mouth. You can feel the sides of your tongue along the inner rim of your upper teeth. Be careful not to overly tense your tongue in ways that are adverse to the free formation of these vowels. There shouldn't be a dip in the blade of the tongue (behind the tip), making it look as if you have an invisible spoon depressing it. A bowled-out tongue can actually make [i] sound like [ɪ].

Vowel modification

In general, as we sing higher, we need greater oral space in order to resonate vowels easily. To accomplish this, vowel modification is a necessity. This means that we make small changes in the position of the vowels as we sing higher (shifting them to the right on the triangle. So an /ee/ would shift toward /ih/. If we were to sing higher and higher, we would ultimately end up on a wide open /ah/ vowel. The same process occurs on the other side of the triangle as well—the little /u/ shifts toward the big /u/, and so on toward /ah/.

One would think that there would be therefore a completely even line showing a general increase in space from the bottom of the voice to the top of the voice, but such is not necessarily the case. Some singers find that, singing lower and lower, there comes a point at which they actually need to begin <u>increasing</u> space in order to get more volume on their lowest notes. See the diagram in the section below.

The Passaggio

In terms of our overall vocal range, the *passaggio* (passageway) is an area of transition or lift from one area of the voice to another, typically medium-high in the range. A singer must make adjustments to the vocal mechanism in order to negotiate the transition (or passage) more smoothly. This can even occur in more than one area of the voice.

Many singers, such as the late Luciano Pavarotti, find that when singing in or through the passaggio, they actually need to <u>reduce</u> space to resonate a vowel most effectively—the "narrowing" feeling occurring in the mouth or the throat.[27] So, their sense of space in singing a scale would look like the next diagram. It increases as an ascending scale is sung, going through an area of reduced space, and then increasing once again to the top. The actual pitch levels at which these transitional changes occur depend on the individual singer—the same as with other characteristics: their vocal weight and timbre (tone color); flexibility and agility; range and tessitura; and even their physical make-up.

Highest notes with greatest space	
Passaggio with narrower space	
Increasing space on ascending scale	
Reducing space on descending scale	
Increasing space at the bottom	

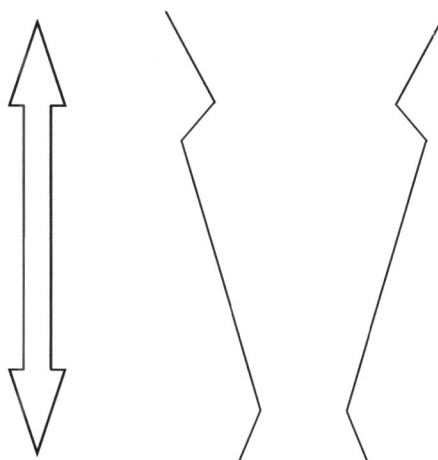

There are <u>many</u> spellings of the /ee/ and /ih/ vowels—several of which involve /e/ and /i/ spellings—including some unusual ones: /ea/ in "each" [itʃ] and the /o/ in "women" ['wɪ mɛn]. Compare and contrast the following words with the [i] and [ɪ] (/ee/ and /ih/) vowels.

Pete	[pit]	pit	[pɪt]
seat	[sit]	picnic	['pɪk nɪk]
beet	[bit]	bit	[bɪt]
genie	['dʒi ni]	gin	[dʒɪn]
heat	[hit]	hit	[hɪt]
leak	[lik]	lick	[lɪk]
keen	[kin]	king	[kɪŋ]

Note that the capital letter in the name Pete isn't accounted for, because it doesn't make a change in the sound of the /p/.

Transcribe the following pairs of words into IPA:

sweet [   ]   quick [   ]

fleece [   ]   flick [   ]

tweet [   ]   twig [   ]

cleat [   ]   click [   ]

Transcribe the following words into their orthographic spellings:

[bik] _____   [tɹit] _____

[slɪk] _____   [slik] _____

[sɪŋ] _____   [fɹʃ] _____

Note: The last two include the /ng/ and /sh/ sounds.

[ɑ] and [æ]	The open /ah/ and short /ă/

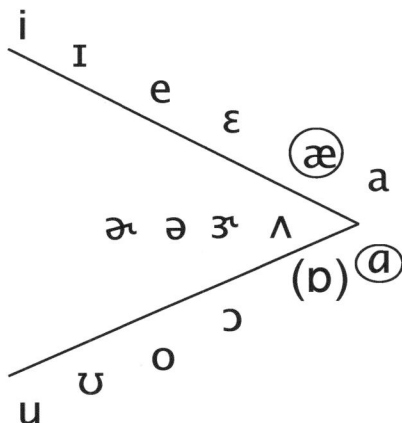

i
 ɪ
  e
   ɛ
    æ
     a
ɚ ə ɝ ʌ ɐ
    (ɒ) ɑ
     ɔ
    o
  ʊ
u

[ɑ]

On the Hellwag triangle, the [ɑ] vowel is the one that, all other things being equal, requires the most vertical space. In singing American English, we use this vowel exclusively whenever the "ah" sound is called for. (A different vowel, [a], is used as the beginning of the long /ī/ diphthong—sometimes seen as the letter /i/ with a macron (the line for the long vowel) over it: /ī/.) Think of the [ɑ] vowel as the one you produce when your doctor says, "Say ah."

A variant of this sound, halfway between /ah/ and /aw/, sounds like a more-rounded form of the /ah/ vowel or a more-open form of the /aw/. It is represented in the International Phonetic Alphabet as a reversed symbol of the "ah" vowel, [ɒ], and is frequently heard in British English and regionalized speech in the United States. It is placed on the ladder in parentheses, because it doesn't necessarily involve actual phonemic identity change (see below) among words in Standard American English; that is, it may act as a chameleon between the two vowels on either side. That said, we want our audiences to be able to decipher between "cot" and "caught" as we sing, so, in order to avoid confusing them, depending on the context, it's better to use the vowels on either side.

The [ɑ] vowel has spellings with both /a/ and /o/ in American English, such as in the words:

hot [hɑt]   When you see the transcription for this word, be careful not to think of what you wear on your head. The vowel in that word ("hat") has a different sound (and, therefore, requires a different vowel in IPA: [hæt]). A distinctly different sound, which can change the meaning of a word if altered, is known as a *phoneme.* Sounds which can be interchanged without altering the meaning of a word are known as *allophones*. For example, it would be a change of phonemic identity to go from "tip" to "top." But whether we sing the word "shirt" with a stopped final /t/ or an exploded /t/, it doesn't change the word's meaning, so these are allophones.

lock [lɑk] Again, be careful not to think of the word "lack" as you look at the transcribed word.

box   [bɑks] Note that the /x/ sound in this word sounds as /k/ and /s/, so those symbols are used in the transcription (putting the word into IPA symbols in brackets). Learn to think in terms of **sound symbols**, rather than letters. As you transcribe a word into IPA, ask yourself, "What are the sounds involved in the singing of this word?" It's a good thing to do also when a word contains a silent letter, such as in the word "knot": [nɑt].

f<u>a</u>ther [ˈfɑ ðɚ]   p<u>a</u>dre [ˈpɑ dɹeɪ] Some words with /a/ spellings such as "f<u>a</u>ther" and "p<u>a</u>dre," and names like B<u>a</u>ch and Br<u>a</u>hms also use the [ɑ] vowel.

[æ]

The short /a/ vowel, often seen as /ă/ in phonetic spellings, and represented by [æ] in IPA, is frequently spelled with the letter /a/, and sometimes in combination with another vowel. It was considered to be the "bad" vowel decades ago,[28] and was avoided in singing—perhaps somewhat influenced by Received Pronunciation (although the [æ] does exist in British speech and song). On the Hellwag triangle, it has almost as much of a need for vertical space as the /ah/ vowel, with a little of the "wide inside" feeling the vowels going toward /ee/ have.

dodge [dɑdʒ]   batch [bætʃ]

Goth   [gɑθ]   hang [hæŋ]

Note: The last one may be different from the way you speak it. Some singers feel or hear the articulatory change toward the /ng/ and sing more of a diphthong, like [heɪŋ]. But that would involve less space in the mouth, plus a forward tongue arch movement for the [ɪ] round-off, rather than a backward tongue arch movement for the /ng/. Work to get the pure vowel (non-diphthong) [æ] into your ear when singing words such as "gang, tangle, pang, mangle, sang," etc.

Now try transcribing these words using one of these four vowels sounds: [i ɪ ɑ æ]

clock	[	]	thin	[	]
plaque	[	]	these	[	]
seas	[	]	seethes	[	]
plaid	[	]	baths	[	]

Note: When a final /s/ comes after a vowel or a voiced consonant, the /s/ is voiced ([z]).

sheep	[	]	shop	[	]
ship	[	]	teeth	[	]
bleak	[	]	with	[	]
blacksmith	[	]	lambs	[	]

Note: It is often advisable to sing the /th/ in the word "with" as a voiced /th/ sound [ð], because it so much easier to project that sound rather than the unvoiced version, [θ]. In the last word, "lambs," remember not to include an IPA symbol for a silent letter.

chock	[	]	thick	[	]
chapped	[	]	beaned	[	]

Now try these words which have more than one syllable, and place an accent mark above and to the left of the stressed syllable. For example, "tricky": [ˈtɹɪ ki]:

mapped   [   ]   chopping   [   ]

picnic   [   ]   Bonnie   [   ]

Write these transcribed words in the their orthographic spelling:

[tʃik]   _____   [fɹɪndʒ]   _____

[dʒæbd]   _____   [fɹæns]   _____

Note: In the last word, avoid inserting a /t/ between the /n/ and /s/. The tendency to insert the /t/ comes from the shift of voicing to unvoicing while in the articulatory position of the blade of the tongue (behind the tip) on the alveolar ridge. The same thing can happen in other articulatory positions, such as bi-labially (both lips), with the name "Clemson" without a /p/).

[θɪŋ]   _____   [ˈsi ɪŋ] _____

[ˈkɪ sɪŋ]   _____   [fɹʃt]   _____

In the last line, note that the first word is syllabified in printed English as "kis-sing," but is sung "kih-sing," the same way in which we see "lov-ing" on the page, but sing it as "luh-ving." These changes allow us to stay on the stressed vowel longer. Remember, it is the vowel that carries the tone.

| [u] and [ʊ] | The long and short "ooh" vowels: /ū/ and /ŭ/ |

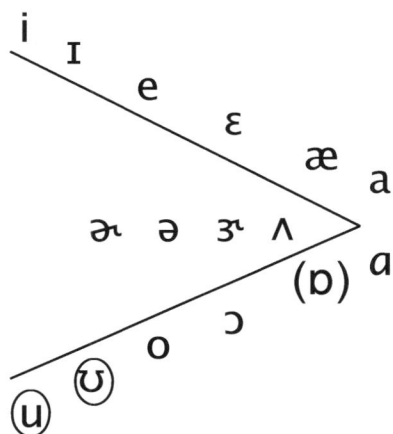

On the Hellwag triangle, the [u] vowel is the one that, all other things being equal, requires the most depth—that is, it feels the furthest "back." It is also the most lip-rounded vowel. The more open form, [ʊ], is deep like the more lip-rounded [u], but needs a little more vertical space, since it is on the way to the most spacious /ah/ vowel at the apex of the triangle. Be careful not to move the tongue arch forward, mixing in an /ee/ vowel. And be careful not to dull the [ʊ] by not rounding the lips enough. Also, remember to allow for some jaw space as well.

The [u] involves the tip of the tongue pulling away from the back of the lower front teeth, and the tongue arching up in the back (thus, a "back" vowel). Because the next vowel up the triangle—the [ʊ] vowel—is closer to [a], this means the [ʊ] vowel has slightly less arch in the back of the tongue. We could then think that the tip of the tongue is therefore slightly farther away from the back of the lower front teeth on [u] than [ʊ].

The action of the lips in forming these vowels is also crucial to making them not only distinguishable, but beautiful as well. Many Americans don't engage their articulators enough in everyday speech, and this can carry over into their singing, making it difficult for the audience to understand the text. Look in a mirror to see how rounded your lips need to be to sing these vowels beautifully. Are they energized enough? Does it <u>look</u> as if you're singing the intended vowel? One nice thing about singing on the stage is that we don't have to do it the way a ventriloquist does. If anything, we should give the audience every advantage in their attempt to understand us, and make the vowels "look like" what they are. Pretend they are almost having to read your lips in order to understand you. Without going overboard with a lot of tension, that's about how energized your articulators should feel, depending on the mood of the song, the genre, etc.

One other characteristic of these two vowels is the amount of vertical space (provided by the jaw position) needed in the mouth. Take a look at the vowel triangle again and compare their relative positions. In my experience as a voice teacher, the [ʊ] vowel seems to be one of the most difficult vowels for students to sing correctly (even if English is their native language). We call the [ʊ] vowel "big /u/," but it's not actually a capital letter, just another IPA symbol.

The [u] vowel is spelled in a variety of ways in American English, such as in the words:

soon	[sun]	flume	[flum]
two	[tu]	shoe	[ʃu]
soup	[sup]	cruise	[kɹuz]

There are also words with the [u] sound like "beauty," ['bju ti], and "few" [fju] which invole the glide [j] before the [u], but we'll learn more about glides in a later chapter. For some words, such as "news," we have a choice in whether or not to use the glide. Singers can consult dictionaries—several excellent ones are available online, such as a website like: http://dictionary.reference.com[29]—or standard works in print, such as Kenyon and Knott's *A Pronouncing Dictionary of American English.*[30]

The [ʊ] vowel is also spelled in a variety of ways in American English, such as in the words:

took [tʊk]	put [pʊt]	should [ʃʊd]

As you sing these words, keep in mind the three crucial things involved in their production: tongue, jaw, and lips. The tongue arches in the back of the mouth, giving it a really deep feeling (and with the tip of the tongue allowed to pull away from the back of the lower front teeth), the jaw still needs to give the vowel some room (Remember the dictum: "All vowels are open"), and the lips should be rounded.

Now practice singing and transcribing these words involving [u] and [ʊ]:

suit   [   ]   boot   [   ]

book   [   ]   coupe   [   ]

flute   [   ]   hoot   [   ]

soot   [   ]   tomb   [   ]

choose   [   ]   Scrooge   [   ]

Note: the last line uses the *affricatives* we saw earlier—[tʃ] for unvoiced, and [dʒ] for voiced.

Transcribe a few more words involving more than one syllable—again, putting the stress mark up and to the left of the accented syllable:

doozy   [   ]   looky!   [   ]

re-hooked   [   ]   Susie   [   ]

booking   [   ]   losing   [   ]

Note: In making a transcription, there's no need for punctuation, hyphens, or capital letters, since you're just writing sound symbols. An apostrophe doesn't actually make a sound, so there's no IPA symbol for it. But if it makes a difference in the way a word is pronounced (mornin' as opposed to morning), then we make a corresponding change in the IPA. A capital letter in the orthographic spelling is sung the same way as its lower case counterpart.

Write these transcribed words in their orthographic spelling:

[tʃuz]   _____   [tɹuθ]   _____

[fʊt]   _____   ['kʊ ki]   _____

['su ðɪŋ]   _____   ['wu zi]   _____

['snu zɪŋ]   _____   [sluθ]   _____

['dʒuk baks]   _____   ['pʊ li]   _____

Here are a few more practice words, using the vowels we've seen thus far. Transcribe them into their orthographic spelling:

[snuzd]   _____   ['ɹuθ lɛs]   _____

[batʃt]   _____   ['kʊ kɪŋ]   _____

[suðd]   _____   [næbd]   _____

['kɪ tʃɛn]   _____   [tɹuθ]   _____

[tʃip]   _____   ['kʊ ʃən]   _____

[eɪ] and [ɛ]	long /ā/ and /eh/

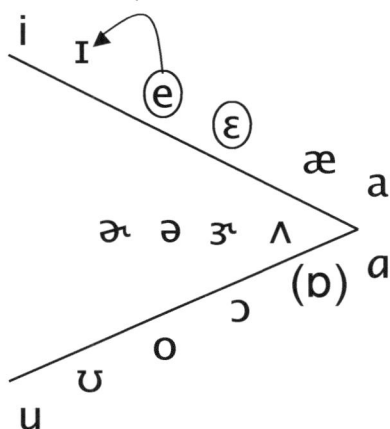

Going back to the upper leg of the triangle, we see the next two vowels actually include our first look at a diphthong—the long /a/ in this case—as well as the /eh/ sound. Note the pronunciation: It sounds like "<u>diff</u>-thong," not "dip-thong."

Diphthongs

A **diphthong** consists of two vowel sounds adjacent to each other within a syllable, forming a new unit. In sustaining pure vowels (non-diphthongs) in singing, we can stay on the vowel for the length of the note. Even if it's followed by a consonant within the syllable, we would typically put the consonant on the next beat, at the end of a phrase. But in a diphthong, we sustain the first (primary) vowel sound, then round off with the second one at the end, either on the release of the note or as we go on to the next sound.

[eɪ] Called "little e, big i"

Let's take a look at our first diphthong in order to visualize that:

day [deɪ] sung as [de.............ɪ]

Even in the plural form, we would sing it similarly, ending with both the round-off and the final consonant:

days [deɪz] sung as [de.............ɪz]

Note: Both of these examples demonstrate how the diphthong is rounded off in classical singing, as opposed to other styles, which tend to round off diphthongs sooner, and often further up the ladder (triangle) toward the little /i/.

Keep in mind that we can sing the diphthong round-offs which go to the /ih/ sound (the diphthongs [aɪ], [eɪ], [ɔɪ], as you will learn later) with a change in the tongue arch, rather than with a change of jaw space also, depending on how high the pitch is. For instance, in a high-pitched phrase, if you were to sing, "I am," having to change the jaw position could make the phrase a lot more difficult to sing (because of still needing space for resonance). But in rounding off the first word and changing to the second word, keeping good space will make singing it easier. This requires independence of the tongue and the jaw.

Independence of Tongue and Jaw

To gain that kind of independence, practice this vocalize in the mirror, watching your tongue. Start with an [i], then change to [ɑ]. Do this several times, and remember that on these vowels you can keep the tip of the tongue at the back of the lower front teeth. Change the amount of arch in the tongue going from one vowel to another. Up for the [i], and back down for the [ɑ]. Now go "ya, ya, ya, ya, ya" on a descending five-note pattern. Try it without moving your jaw—maintaining an open (tall) position. The vertical oval shape of the mouth is really an ideal one for most phrases. There's no need to tense the jaw to get it to stop moving though. Now alternate between [ɑ] and the [ɪ] vowel. Do this several times, paying attention to a quiet jaw and a freely arching tongue. Try it by singing the words, "I am," "I am," "I am." Notice how the tongue can do the work of rounding off the diphthong in the word "I," rather than having the jaw help. Now sing the phrase on a medium pitch, then medium-high, then an even higher note. Gaining control of your articulators is well worth the effort.

The [eɪ] diphthong is spelled in a variety of ways in American English, such as in these homonyms:

raise	[ɹeɪz]	rays	[ɹeɪz]
way	[weɪ]	weigh	[weɪ]
Hey!	[heɪ]	hay	[heɪ]
rain	[ɹeɪn]	reign	[ɹeɪn]

The Choral [e] and [o]

Some schools of thought—probably more among choral directors than voice teachers—dictate that long /a/ is a pure vowel, rather than diphthongs, perhaps feeling that a large ensemble of voices can blend more easily by not having to migrate away from the primary vowel sound. Some even close the primary vowel in this diphthong, making it so closed that there's no need for a round-off. They've often already gone <u>beyond</u> the round-off vowel, and it doesn't sound much like American English. Perhaps they've been influenced by Italian's smaller vowel set, in which the closed / e/ is indeed a pure, non-diphthong vowel. Or is it because the primary and secondary vowels of the diphthong are next to each other on the vowel triangle? Or maybe it's the difficulty of the change of vowel on higher pitches If you direct a choral group, try doing a true diphthong on long /a/ and vowel. If the group can blend and articulate together on the other diphthongs like long /ī/, or in a word like "toys," perhaps they can sing [eɪ] also, especially at lower pitch levels.

[ɛ]

The next vowel down the upper leg of the triangle is called "epsilon" (from the Greek alphabet), with the phonetic spelling /eh/, as in "let." In terms of jaw space and tongue arch, we're almost at the half-way point between /ah/ and /ee/. The tip of the tongue should be at the back of the lower front teeth. Typical spellings involve the letter /e/, sometimes in combination with other vowels, as in:

let	[lɛt]	breath	[bɹɛθ]
bluebell	['blu bɛɫ]	wealth	[wɛɫθ]
stepped	[stɛpt]	ebbs	[ɛbz]

Now practice singing and transcribing these words involving [eɪ] and [ɛ]:

pay day	[ ]	tend	[ ]
paid	[ ]	said	[ ]
fled	[ ]	head	[ ]
changed	[ ]	faded	[ ]

Note: The last word actually uses both of these vowels. The epsilon, [ɛ], because it is in an unstressed syllable, doesn't need to sound as bright as when it is accented. Some phonetics texts will then add a diacritic or another symbol, such as a superscript schwa, to the [ɛ], which looks like [ɛ^ə], indicating a mixture of vowels (or a "tinged" vowel). Two ways to see this change are on the triangle itself. We could either say that the accented and unaccented epsilons are shown with a couple of arrows on the epsilon, like so:

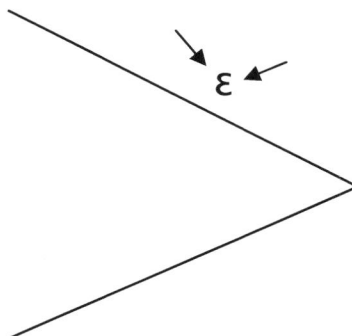

In this case, the accented version can be thought of as being a little higher on the triangle, with the tongue arched slightly more. The unaccented one can be thought of as being a little lower on the triangle, with the tongue arched slightly less. The difficulty with this thinking is that this would imply that the unstressed vowel has more jaw space, since it's a little further to the right on the triangle. But such is not the case, because the unstressed vowel might actually have less space that the stressed one. So, where to show it on the triangle? Take a look at the diagram below, and you'll see an arrow indicating the spot of mixture between the epsilon and the schwa.

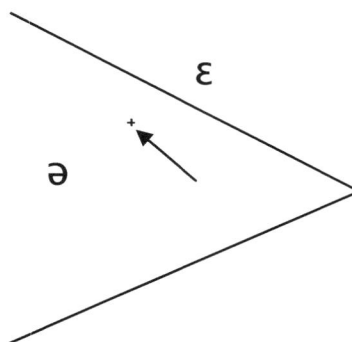

So, we indicate the vowel in the IPA with the epsilon, but feel that it gets "tinged" with the schwa, making it less bright: [ɛ^ə]. That way the audience doesn't hear the word "faded" as containing the word "dead" in the second syllable.

Practice this by singing the following words, putting the vowel in the unstressed syllable between the epsilon and the schwa:

baited mistreated seeded

Using the right amount of consonant energy based on where a consonant falls in a word—initial, medial, final—also helps the audience's understanding. For instance, in the first word, we wouldn't want them to hear the words "bay Ted," or in the second word, "mystery Ted," or "see dead" in the third word. Can you hear and feel the differences—both the vowel in the second syllable, and the medial consonant—between "seeded" and "see dead"? Again, we want to give our audience every advantage we can in being able to understand us, and making these slight shadings of vowels and differences in the amount of energy in the consonants can help greatly.

Sing and write these transcribed words in their orthographic spelling:

[tʃɛkt] _____ [fleɪkt] _____

[ˈlɛŋ θɛn] _____ [ˈseɪ ɪŋ] _____

[ˈteɪ stɛd] _____ [ɛm ˈbɛ ɹəst] _____

Note: In the fourth word, "saying," we don't actually close all the way to the /y/ sound in the middle of the word (as if the second syllable were "ying," but instead gently round off the diphthong. Another pronunciation for the last example, "embarrassed," in some dictionaries is with the vowel [æ] in the second syllable: [ɛm ˈbæ ɹəst]. While this vowel is heard more in the northeast, both vowels are used nationwide, and the majority of people may actually put the sound between the [æ] and the [ɛ] without really thinking about which one they're using. The same is true for other words spelled with /ar/: "carry," "marry," "tarry," and the names "Barry," "Harry," "Larry," "Mary," etc. Words and names with other spellings in the accented syllable, for instance /er/, usually go with the [ɛ] sound: "ferry," "Sherry," and even "dairy."

Also, rather than using an [ɪ] vowel for the third syllable of "embarrassed," we go with a schwa. Whether a syllable is accented or unaccented, try to take the spelling of the word into consideration for which vowel is chosen. For instance, in the word "perfect," (noun, as opposed to verb), the vowel in the second syllable comes somewhere between the epsilon and the schwa. The epsilon is a type of /e/ spelling, but in order to make an [ɪ] sound, there would need to be some sort of an /i/ in the orthographic spelling.

Here are more words for you to sing and transcribe into IPA:

flattened	[ ]	flexed	[	]
entailed	[ ]	filthy	[	]
foxtrot	[ ]	cooking	[	]
suited	[ ]	hooked	[	]
soothing	[ ]	jaded	[	]
chapped	[ ]	guestbook	[	]
staying	[ ]	icky	[	]
jinxed	[ ]	props	[	]
sobs	[ ]	pulleys	[	]
cruise	[ ]	fetch	[	]
saddened	[ ]	batch	[	]
indigestion	[ ]	tapping	[	]
box top	[ ]	village	[	]

impaled   [   ]   Jackie   [   ]

maiden   [   ]   flocks   [   ]

pay day   [   ]   swigged   [   ]

gymnasium [   ]   cheeky   [   ]

[ɔ] and [oʊ]	Open and closed /o/: /aw/ and /oh/

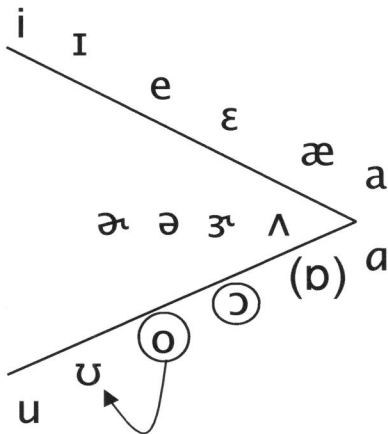

Completing the lower leg of the triangle, we come to the open and closed /o/ vowels. Like the long /ā/, the long /ō/ is also a diphthong, moving from an initial position—the primary vowel [o]—to a round-off position—the secondary vowel [ʊ]. Be sure not to round off too far to the closed /u/ sound. Also, remember to sustain the /o/ for the almost the entire length of the note, then round off at the release, or when going into the oncoming sound on the next pitch.

As with other sounds, these vowels can have degrees of roundedness, or brightness and darkness. These shadings can also be represented with diacritics in the IPA, and they can even be further noted and studied on the vowel triangle with the placement of arrows showing how far left-to-right the vowel is actually being sung. Keep in mind that vowels are not "digital" in position—that is, our voices and articulators are "analog." Unlike a piano, we can "play in the cracks," and make all of the infinite shadings required to make a vowel sound just right. As we saw before, we can even mix a schwa (in the middle of the triangle) into our sound. Using your ears, even recording yourself, you can create a wide variety of sounds that are not only beautiful, but which communicate easily as well.

[oʊ]

As mentioned with the [eɪ] diphthong, many choral singers are instructed not to round off the long /ō/, but to sing a pure vowel (non-diphthong) instead. Again, this isn't really American English, but an influence from other languages such as Italian. Like the [eɪ] diphthong, the movement from primary to secondary vowel in this diphthong is minimal, as seen in the short, curved arrow in the diagram above. With the [oʊ] diphthong, as we saw with the [eɪ], we sustain the primary vowel, then round off with the secondary one. Thus, we find:

own [oʊn] sung as [o...........ʊn]

Even with the word "owns," we would sing it similarly, ending with both the round-off and the final consonants:

owns [oʊnz] sung as [o...........ʊnz]

Note: Again, both of these examples demonstrate how the diphthong is rounded off in classical singing, as opposed to other styles, which tend to round off diphthongs sooner, and often further along the ladder (triangle) toward the little /u/.

Typical spellings of this diphthong are with an /o/, sometimes in combination with other vowels:

home [hoʊm] comb [koʊm]

grown [gɹoʊn] loan [loʊn]

The words "boat" and "pole" both use the diphthong [oʊ]. They may feel like different sounds, since we tend to take the /l/ sound in a dark/back-of-the-mouth direction, but they are actually the same diphthong. Keeping the [oʊ] more forward than normal can help it not to be too dark in anticipation of the oncoming /l/, and for the /l/ not to be too dark as well, as it might tend to be in [pol]. Instead, use [poʊl] or [poʊɫ].

[ɔ]

On the Hellwag triangle, the open /o/ vowel is almost as spacious as the pure /ah/ in terms of jaw opening, but has more rounding of the lips and a feeling of some depth, as it is on the side of the triangle which leads to /u/ at the end. Interestingly, singers who tend to prefer rounded lips on almost all vowels sometimes substitute this vowel for the sound of pure /ah/. Likewise, some singers substitute (ɒ) or [ɑ] or [a] for [ɔ] in some words (even little words like "on"), not realizing the regionalized accent they are using. In the South, some pronounce "on" as "own," and in the North, it is often heard as "ahn." Phonemic changes like this can potentially create some humorous misunderstandings for the audience. Try singing the following words in rows, and listen for the differences in the vowels and feeling the differences in jaw space and lip rounding:

[ɑ]	[ɔ]	[oʊ]
cot	caught	coat
sod	sawed	sowed
tot	taught	tote
hottie	haughty	Terre <u>Haute</u> [hoʊt]

If you find yourself thinking, "But those two are the same sound," keep working to be able to distinguish the finer points of these vowels. Perhaps even exaggerate them at first, in order to hear the differences. Give yourself time, keeping an open mind (and ear). Remember, we want your ears to "grow" through this process.

Typical spellings of this vowel are with an /o/, but /au/, /aw/, and others are frequently seen also.

Now practice singing and transcribing these words using [ɔ] and [oʊ]:

pose	[	]	pause	[	]
cough	[	]	paws	[	]
thought	[	]	though	[	]
blown	[	]	blow	[	]
chosen	[	]	flawed	[	]

66

Sing and transcribe these words using [ɔ], [a], and [oʊ]:

body   [   ]   bawdy   [   ]

bought   [   ]   boating   [   ]

throat   [   ]   throttle   [   ]

oddly   [   ]   oatmeal   [   ]

taupe   [   ]   cop   [   ]

fought   [   ]   con   [   ]

taught   [   ]   docks   [   ]

boxed   [   ]   coaxed   [   ]

jokes   [   ]   coach   [   ]

naughty   [   ]   knot   [   ]

Write these transcribed words in their orthographic spelling:

[tʃapt]   _____

['loʊn li]   _____

['plɔ zɪ bɫ]   _____

[flɔd]   _____

['tʃɪ kɛn ˌpaks]   _____

[poʊtʃt]   _____

The schwa and hooked schwa pairs: [ʌ] [ə] and [ɝ] [ɚ]	"central" or "neutral" vowels: /uh/ and /er/

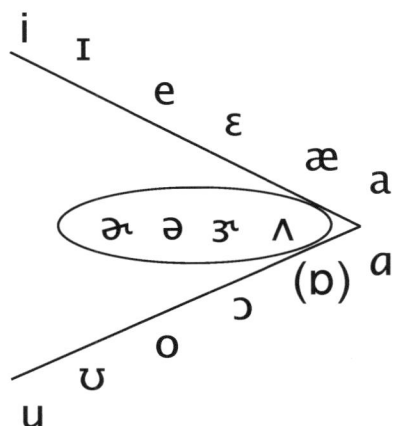

The four central or neutral vowels are placed in the middle of the triangle. They come in pairs, both accented and unaccented:

accented /uh/: [ʌ]

unaccented /uh/: [ə]

accented /er/: [ɝ]

unaccented /er/: [ɚ]

We can relate them to the vowel /ah/ from Hellwag's triangle. Slowly sing [a] and [ʌ], and go back and forth between them. The vertical space required by [ʌ] is nearly the same, but not quite as great. Another way to hear and feel the slight difference between the two is to sing "above" and then change it to "uh-BAHV." There is indeed a difference, and it may seem ridiculous to sing "uh-BAHV," but, remember that decades ago, the schwa was looked down on (considered the "dull" vowel), and /ah/ was the prescribed pronunciation, much as [æ] (called the "bad" vowel)[31] was substituted with [a]. Of course, I tell my students: "There are no bad vowels—only inept execution"—a take-off of the Dorothy Uris maxim regarding "ugly consonants."[32]

Actually, the word "above" is a perfect example of how to feel the difference between the accented and unaccented schwa. Look in the mirror as you sing it. Can you see the greater space for the vowel in the second syllable? Here's the transcription in IPA: [ə ˈbʌv].

Try this vocal exercise on a sustained pitch. Going back and forth among the vowels [a], [ʌ], and [ə]:

[a]   [ʌ]   [ə]   [ʌ]   [a]   [ʌ]   [ə]   [ʌ]   [a]

Feel the slight jaw differences. Both the tongue and the lips remain neutral, relaxed, unless we're coloring the sound by means of different shaping. So, the main difference between the /ah/ and the schwa vowels is vertical height—that is, as always, the jaw space in combination with the distance between the top of the tongue and the roof of the mouth.

[ʌ] and [ə]   Accented and unaccented schwa

There are many potential spellings for the accented and unaccented schwa vowels. In an accented syllable, it will often be spelled with a /u/ or a vowel combination with /u/. Unaccented, many spellings drop to the schwa in our speech. Consider this, the unaccented schwa is the most frequently heard sound in spoken English. (And I don't mean speakers who constantly say, "Uh…"). For singing, when we can put a vowel "on" on the ladder (that is, on one of the legs of the triangle), we should probably do it—even if we have to consider that vowel as "tinged" (or tinted) by the schwa. Again, look at the spelling of the word. Is it spelled with an /e/? It might go to the epsilon. Is it spelled with an /i/? It might go to the big /i/, and so forth. Use your ear—your ever-developing, ever-growing ear.

The difference in the accented and unaccented schwa can be heard in singing the name "Landon Dunn." The first name ends with an unstressed syllable (the regular schwa), and the last name uses the stressed version. In singing the name, we use a much more open jaw space (depending on pitch) for the third syllable than the second syllable.

Landon Dunn   [ˈlæn dən dʌn]

Here is an example of the unaccented schwa in contrast to putting the sound on the ladder instead:

carrot [ˈkɛ ɹət] (or [ˈkæ ɹət])   but   sonnet   [ˈsɑ nɛt]

Note: In both of these words, some dictionaries recommend an /ih/ sound in the second syllable ([ɪ] in the IPA). But this is really a more closed tongue position (the arch high in the front) than necessary. The epsilon (perhaps tinged with schwa) communicates very clearly and is more open for singing.

Of course, the unaccented syllable with a vowel change away from schwa doesn't always occur at the end of the word, as shown in these two:

cinnamon   [ˈsɪ nə mən]   but   beautiful   [ˈbju tɪ fəɬ]

In the last example, note that the middle syllable can go to the /ih/ sound, rather than simply dropping to a schwa as in speech. The argument could even be made for changing the vowel in the last syllable to a big /u/ sound, as in "full." Part of that may depend on the musical setting of the text: how long will the last syllable be sustained, and on how high a pitch? How are the relative dynamics of the three syllables? Of course, we could also call it a "tinge" vowel, and put the big /u/ with the superscript schwa in the IPA transcription: [ʊᵊ].

Stressed or unstressed?

For monosyllabic (one-syllable) words, a choice will have to be made regarding whether the schwa is stressed or unstressed. A lot of the decision will come from the context—how important is the part of speech? How important did the composer seem to think the word was, as represented by pitch, duration, meter, etc.? For instance, if the one-syllable word is "but," it could be an everyday conjunction. However, if the word "but" could potentially negate everything I've just been singing about, it might be a really important word, and could get the [ʌ] vowel, rather than the simple unaccented schwa [ə]. Normally, an active verb or a descriptive adjective would get more stress, but an indefinite article like "a" would probably not. For example, in the phrase, "I met a man from Tennessee," the word "a" would be sung with an unaccented schwa (and not with a long /a/ either.)

Now practice singing and transcribing these words using [ʌ] and [ə]:

rebuttal   [   ]   ruckus   [   ]

roughage   [   ]   toughness   [   ]

fungus   [   ]   among   [   ]

bluffing   [   ]   blustery   [   ]

handcuffed   [   ]   bunches   [   ]

70

thumbs	[ ]	honey	[ ]
muddy	[ ]	pickup	[ ]
bubbled	[ ]	gushed	[ ]
teacup	[ ]	cutting	[ ]

Sing and write these transcribed words in their orthographic spelling:

[tʃʌkt] _____

[ən ə 'bæʃt] _____

['pʌmp kɪn] _____

[əm 'bɹɛ lə] _____

['lʌntʃ ɹum] _____

['pʌn tɛᵊd] _____

[ɝ] and [ɚ] Accented and unaccented hooked schwa

The hooked schwa vowels, while paired as accented and unaccented forms, are quite different from the regular schwa pair. Although some textbooks advocate otherwise,[33] the tip of the tongue is pulled away from the back of the lower front teeth and bent down toward the floor of the mouth (not retroflexed like the American hard /r/ consonant), and the lips are brought in at the corners. This really can be a quite beautiful sound. Again, remember the dictum: "There are no bad vowels—just inept execution." (Come to think of it, we could actually make any vowel sound bad, if we tried hard enough!)

Some good examples of words with both vowels are:

learner ['lɝ nɚ]   Turner ['tɝ nɚ]   burner ['bɝ nɚ]

Note: When these words stand alone or end a phrase, the American hard /r/ (consonant) doesn't occur, the same as when the unstressed hooked schwa occurs as a diphthong round-off. We don't need to flip the tongue up in a retroflex position then.

Watch your tongue in a mirror. Can you sing the word "cursor" without your tongue coming up for the two /r/ sounds? (The jaw does close somewhat for the /s/). There's no need to insert a hard /r/ in there at all. This could be a Scottish remnant in some parts of the country. Some speech regionalisms in American English use a flipped /r/ sound, [ɾ], in a final [ɚ], even changing the vowel to a schwa. When singing, always be aware of the vowel you're going for, as well as any extra movement of the tongue. We would, however, add the American hard /r/ when linking into an oncoming vowel.

Sing: ever ['ɛ vɚ]   rather than ['ɛ vəɾ]

In a musical phrase, we might sing, "Take another turn!" using the unstressed hooked schwa for "anoth<u>er</u>" and the stressed schwa for "turn." There are many spellings of these vowels, as shown in the examples below. For the monosyllables, see the discussion on stressed and unstressed schwa to determine which symbol should be used.

Here are some examples of words using the stressed and unstressed schwa:

thirsty	[ˈθɝ sti]	athirst	[ə ˈθɝst]
bothered	[ˈbɑ ðɚd]	worship	[ˈwɝ ʃɪp]
thirty	[ˈθɝ ti]	Schirmer	[ˈʃɝ mɚ]
heard	[hɝd]	encourage	[ɛn ˈkɝ rɪdʒ]
southern	[ˈsʌ ðɚn]	further	[ˈfɝ ðɚ]

Note: In the word "encourage," we use both the accented hooked schwa and the hard American /r/, just as in the words "curry," "hurry," and "surrey," rather than singing, "huh-ry" like [ˈhʌ ri]. We actually need both sounds—the vowel influenced by the oncoming /r/, and the /r/ itself. This is similar to some /ng/ spellings in which the [ŋ] symbol is present as well as the hard /g/—for example, "hunger" [ˈhʌŋ gɚ].

Remember that in terms of greatest to least vertical oral space, the four vowels occur on the triangle in the order of:

ʌ	ɝ	ə	ɚ

Look again at the chart of these vowels a few pages back. This isn't the way they've usually been represented in textbooks, but is actually the way we sing them, in terms of the amount of jaw space. Again, moving from left to right on the chart indicates that, everything else being equal, there is an increase in oral space—a dropping of the jaw.[34]

Now practice singing and transcribing these words:

unworthy	[	]	colonel	[	]
jumper	[	]	butter churn	[	]
myrrh	[	]	color	[	]
another	[	]	collar	[	]
slumbered	[	]	cummerbund	[	]
ermine	[	]	furthered	[	]
eastern	[	]	custard	[	]
burglary	[	]	jerked	[	]
customers	[	]	cutlery	[	]
quirky	[	]	urked	[	]
perjury	[	]	thunder	[	]

Now sing and write these transcribed words in their orthographic spelling:

['blʌ di ɚ] _____

['dʌz n̩t] _____

[ən 'lʌ ki] _____

[ən 'fɝ·ld] _____

['plʌ mɚ] _____

['fɝ nɪʃt] _____

Diphthongs	**Chapter 6**

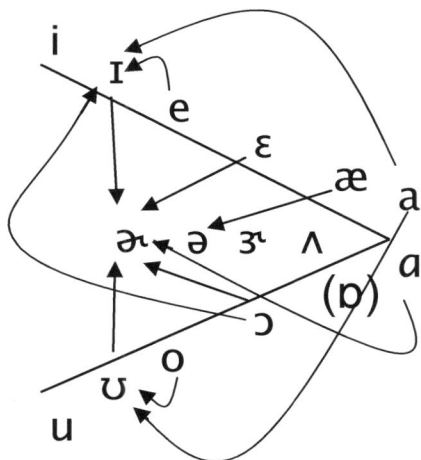

As stated in an earlier chapter, the term *diphthong* means two vowel sounds adjacent to each other within one syllable. Therefore, as you can probably guess, a *triphthong* is <u>three</u> vowel sounds within a syllable.

Thus far, we've only discussed two of the diphthongs, [eɪ] and [oʊ]. In this chapter and the next, we add the rest, [aɪ], [ɔɪ], [aʊ], [ɪɚ], [ɛɚ], [ɑɚ], [ɔɚ], [ʊɚ], and [æə]., as well as the triphthongs [aɪɚ] and [aʊɚ].

While the diagram to the left almost looks like a football play on a locker room chalkboard, it will be easier to grasp, when you realize that there are only four vowel sounds that are used as the secondary vowel round-offs:. two with [ɪ], two with [ʊ], five with [ɚ], and one with [ə]. Various diction texts through the years have numbered the diphthongs differently, from as few as five to the present text with   eleven.[35]

[aɪ] and [ɔɪ]   Long /ī/ and /oy/

The first diphthong we studied was [eɪ]. It rounded off not quite all the way to the end of the upper leg of the triangle. There are two more which round off to the [ɪ]: [aɪ] and [ɔɪ], the long /ī/ and /oy/ sounds.

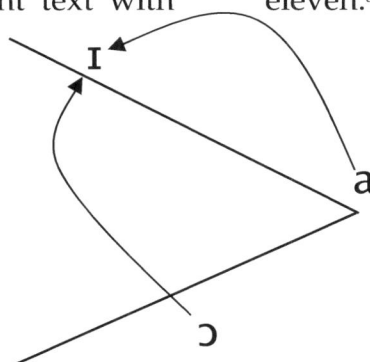

First of all, notice that the symbol for the long /ī/ diphthong begins with a different looking /a/ symbol. See it on the diagram of the vowel ladder above? It's on the other side of the apex of the triangle. This is brighter than the /ah/ sound in the word "father," but the tongue arch isn't as far forward as for the [æ] vowel. We use both the brighter and darker /ah/ sounds in French and German as well, with the same IPA symbols: [a] and [ɑ].

There are various spellings of the long /ī/, as shown in the examples below. As you sing these words, remember to sustain the primary vowel (bright /ah/) for the length of the note, then round off with the secondary vowel (/ih/) at the end. As you see in the diagram, the [aɪ] and the [aʊ] diphthongs involve the greatest amount of movement of the tongue—almost the entire width of the triangle.

Here are some examples of the [aɪ] diphthong:

I'll	[aɪl]	aisle	[aɪl]	while	[hwaɪl]
height	[haɪt]	Haydn	['haɪ dn̩]	geyser	['gaɪ zɚ]
night	[naɪt]	bye	[baɪ]	white	[hwaɪt]
pie	[paɪ]	eyes	[aɪz]	triad	['tɹaɪ æd]

The [ɔɪ] diphthong involves a lot of movement of the articulators. Think about it—we're moving from one side of the vowel triangle to the other, so the tongue movement goes from slightly arched in the back of the mouth to greatly arched in the front of the mouth. The lips move from being slightly engaged to not ordinarily being a part of the vowel formation. And the jaw is much more open for the primary vowel than for the secondary one.

There are two main spellings of the [ɔɪ] diphthong: /oi/ and /oy/. When singing some non-standard American English accents, we may encounter words like "time" or "purse," and use an exaggerated [ɔɪ] diphthong there as well.

Here are some examples of the standard spellings:

toys	[tɔɪz]	Hoyle	[hɔɪɫ]

foiled   [fɔɪɫd]   annoyed [ə 'nɔɪd]

poison   ['pɔɪ zən]   coy   [kɔɪ]

noisy   ['nɔɪ zi]   oily   ['ɔɪ li]

Transcribe the following words using [aɪ] and [ɔɪ] into IPA:

hiding	[ ]	pied	[ ]
foiled	[ ]	joyous	[ ]
Ohio	[ ]	ply	[ ]
royal	[ ]	loiter	[ ]
cycle	[ ]	tricycle	[ ]

Now practice transcribing these words in their orthographic spelling:

['tʃɔɪ sɛz] _____   ['naɪt: taɪm] _____

['paɪ θan] _____   [sɔɪɫ] _____

[sɔɪ sɔs] _____   ['naɪ lan] _____

['taɪ gɚ] _____   ['vɔɪ ɪdʒ] _____

Note: The colon used in the second example indicates the elongation of the sound preceding the colon. In this case, the first /t/ is stopped (some would even say "imploded"), and the second /t/ is exploded. In a sense, they become one long /t/, rather than being two popped or exploded consonants, called a "double drumbeat."

[aʊ]

The [aʊ] diphthong, like the [ɔɪ], involves a great deal of movement of the jaw, tongue, and lips. Notice how the initial vowel of the diphthong is the brighter of the two /ah/ vowels, rather than the darker. Contrast this with an imitation of the heavy Austrian-accented "Terminator" hitting his elbow on a table: "Ow" then would sound like [ɑʊ], as we see in some German diction texts. Parenthetically, in the speech of many Americans, tension in the initial vowel makes it go almost to the [æ] sound—or even [eɪ].

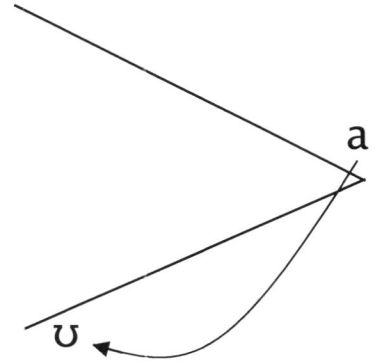

The most frequent spellings for the [aʊ] diphthong are /ou/ and /ow/, as seen in several of the examples below:

pound [paʊnd]   cow   [kaʊ]   coward ['kaʊ ɚd]

cacao [kə 'kaʊ]   joust [dʒaʊst]   power   ['paʊ ɚ]

Note: In the word "power," the /w/ is silent. If "power" has only one note set to it, or if it appears in the music as "pow'r," it may be thought of as a triphthong, which we'll find out more about later.

Transcribe the following words, most using [aʊ], into IPA:

downtown   [   ]   found   [   ]

counted   [   ]   dowry   [   ]

flounder   [   ]   flown   [   ]

Note: Careful with that last one!

Now try transcribing these words into their orthographic spelling:

['kɹaʊ dɛd] _____   [klaʊd] _____

['kaʊ bɔɪ] _____   [saʊθ] _____

[ˈmɔɪ sɛᵊn] _____   [ˈɔɪ stɚz] _____

[ˈtɹaʊ zɚz] _____   [ˈtaʊ ɚɫ] _____

Note: In the last word, the /w/ in the orthographic spelling isn't actually pronounced, like the /w/ in "power."

The six [ɚ] and [ə] diphthongs

There are five diphthongs in American English which round off with the [ɚ] vowel as well as one with the schwa. These are: [ɪɚ], [ɛɚ], [ɑɚ], [ɔɚ], [ʊɚ], and [æə].

[æə]

The [æə] diphthong is rather exceptional, in that it is contained in the slang word "yeah," which we occasionally get to sing. (Note: this is pronouncing the word "yeah" as [jæə], and not [jeɪ], which is spelled more often "yay," or even "yea.") The move from the primary to the secondary vowel is a slight one—the least movement of any of these six diphthongs. But the very slight forward tongue arch drops at the round-off, as the jaw space diminishes for the neutral schwa.

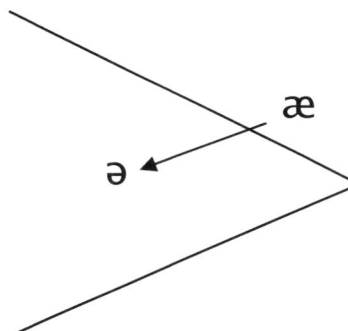

[ɪɚ]

All of the spellings of the hooked schwa diphthongs involve an /r/. As with other diphthongs, we sustain the primary vowel and round off with the secondary one, the [ɚ]. First, let's take a look at the [ɪɚ] diphthong. The primary vowel involves an arched tongue with the tip at the back of the lower front teeth. Some speakers use an [i] vowel to begin this diphthong, but it doesn't have to be so tense. The /ih/ sound will allow your diphthong to be

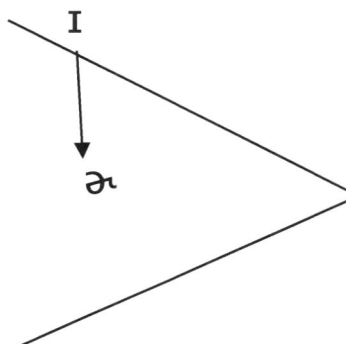

more open. We round off with the [ɚ] by releasing the tongue arch, simultaneously dipping the tip of the tongue down toward the gum ridge behind the lower front teeth and slightly pulling in the corners of the mouth.

Sing "hear" as: [hɪ.............ɚ]

rather than [hi..............ɚ]

There are a few different spellings, as seen below:

mere [mɪɚ]   pier [pɪɚ]   deer [dɪɚ]

fear [fɪɚ]   near [nɪɚ]   sear [sɪɚ]

Note that the last word is different from the word "seer," which goes into two syllables (like /see-er/), and would look like ['si ɚ] in the IPA, breaking syllabically like the word "seeing": ['si ɪŋ].

The next example may seem difficult (or wrong) at first, but perhaps by this time in the text, your ears are able to catch the correct sounds. The word "hero" can be transcribed this way:

hero   ['hɪɚ ɹoʊ]   or even ['hɪ ɹoʊ]   depending on the tempo.

Why would we choose the "big I," rather than "little i"? Think about it for a moment, and sound it out. Would we actually sing it as "he row"? The "big i" sound /ih/ is more open (and is the first vowel of this diphthong anyway). Notice also that the word contains the "American hard /r/" as well as the round-off hooked schwa of the diphthong. Going into the oncoming vowel (the final diphthong in the word), we have to retroflex the tongue. Practice singing it slowly until it feels natural to you. Try it also with the word "zero."

Transcribe the following words, many using the [ɪɚ] diphthong, into IPA:

hearing [   ]   teardrop   [   ]

beard [   ]   ears   [   ]

cheer [   ]   heard   [   ]

Note: Again, careful with that last one!

Now try transcribing these words into their orthographic spelling:

[ɹɪɚd] _____   [ɛn ˈdɪɚd] _____

[tɪɚ] _____   [nɪɚ] _____

[dʒɪɚ] _____   [stɪɚ] _____

Note: Keep in mind that, in the context of singing a phrase, the sound of the hooked schwa may change to the hard /r/ consonant in the link, like so: "ear and eye" is actually sung more like [ɪ‿ɹæn‿daɪ], with the /r/ and /d/ getting less energy than regular initial consonants would, since they're linked (thus, acting medially). We see here that the diphthong is then missing in the word "ear," again depending on the tempo, as the /r/ sound is now thrown over to the next syllable. The slower the tempo, the more time we have to round off the diphthong before the /r/.

[ɛɚ]

As with the [ɪɚ] diphthong, we sustain the primary vowel [ɛ] and round off with the [ɚ]. The primary vowel involves a somewhat arched tongue with the tip at the back of the lower front teeth. One difficulty many speakers have with the [ɛɚ] diphthong is changing it to /āy-er/, that is, breaking it into two syllables. Singing [ɛɚ] allows the diphthong to be smoother, and appropriately monosyllabic. We round off with the [ɚ] by releasing the forward tongue arch, simultaneously dipping the tip of the tongue down toward the gum ridge behind the lower front teeth and slightly pulling in the corners of the mouth.

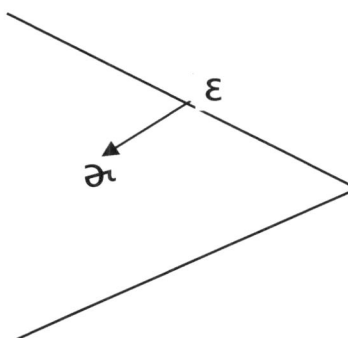

Sing "hair" as: [hɛ...............ɚ]

rather than [heɪ.............ɚ]

There are a few different spellings, as seen below:

bare	[bɛɚ]	bear	[bɛɚ]
fare	[fɛɚ]	fair	[fɛɚ]
share	[ʃɛɚ]	ne'er	[nɛɚ]
wear	[wɛɚ]	care	[kɛɚ]

Note: the first row of words contains homonyms (words that sound exactly alike even though they are spelled differently). The poetic word "ne'er" (not pronounced like "near") is seen in songs as a contraction for "never," so the IPA is like "never," just with the /v/ missing, and in one syllable, rather than two.

Another note: As stated previously with the [ɪɚ] diphthong, in the context of singing a legato phrase, the sound of the hooked schwa may change to the hard /r/ consonant in a legato link. With the [ɛɚ] diphthong, the phrase "air and water" becomes [ɛ ɹænd 'wɑ tɚ], with the /r/ getting less energy than a normal initial consonant, since it's linked and acting as a medial. Once again, the diphthong is then potentially missing in the word "air," as the /r/ sound is in the next syllable.

Transcribe the following words, using the [ɛɚ] diphthong, into IPA:

dared	[	]	there	[	]
chair	[	]	mare	[	]
glare	[	]	hair and eyes	[	]

Note: The word "hair" also changes in its adjective form. The word "hairy," in two syllables, uses the hard American /r/ to begin a second syllable, thus: ['hɛ ɹi].

Now try transcribing these words into their orthographic spelling:

[ɹɛɚ] _____   [ɪm 'pɛɚd] _____

[stɛɚz] _____   [skɛɚd] _____

[flɛɚ] _____   [skwɛɚ] _____

[aɚ]

As with the other diphthongs rounding off with the [ɚ] vowel, in the [aɚ] we sustain the primary vowel and round off with the [ɚ]. The primary vowel here involves a relatively flat tongue position, with the tip at the back of the lower front teeth. We round off with the [ɚ] by dipping the tip of the tongue down toward the gum ridge behind the lower front teeth and slightly pulling in the corners of the mouth. This diphthong is often, but not always, spelled /ar/, as seen below:

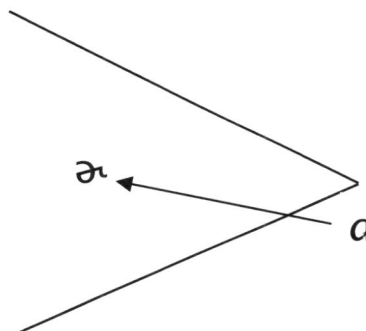

car   [kaɚ]   far   [faɚ]   heart   [haɚt]

shard   [ʃaɚd]   chart [tʃaɚt]   barred   [baɚd]

Transcribe the following words, using the [aɚ] diphthong, into IPA:

darted   [   ]   jar   [   ]

charred   [   ]   mar   [   ]

stars   [   ]   nard   [   ]

Transcribe these words from IPA into their orthographic spelling:

[ˈpɑɚ ti] _____   [kɑɚts] _____

[ˈstɑɚ tɚ] _____   [ˈhɑɚ pɪst] _____

[ˈfɑɚ ðɚ] _____   [ˈskɑɚ fɪŋ] _____

Note: Listen closely, and watch your tongue in the mirror, as you sing the vowels ending in the hooked schwa. Do you go to a retroflex /r/ or even a flipped /r/ at the end instead? Some singers are unaware that they do this, but again, it sounds more like a Scottish accent.

Also, as we saw with the [ɪɚ] and [ɛɚ] diphthongs, in the context of singing a legato phrase, the sound of the hooked schwa may change to the hard /r/ consonant in the link. With the [ɑɚ] diphthong, the phrase "are ever" becomes [ɑ ˈɹɛ vɚ], with the /r/ in the word "are" getting less energy than a regular initial consonant, since it's linked and acting as a medial consonant. Again, the diphthong is then missing in the word "are," as the /r/ is linked into the next syllable.

[ɔɚ]

The next diphthong, [ɔɚ], can be a tricky one in the ears of many singers. That might be because there's no diphthong with an IPA of [oɚ], but they've been used to singing words like "horse" with a more closed sound for the initial vowel of the diphthong. The only problem is, that breaks the word into two syllables. Think about it: the sounds of [oɚ] are almost the way we would pronounce words like "mower," or "rower," "thrower," etc. It's close to it, because there's actually already a diphthong in the first syllable in that case: [oʊ]. For example, someone who owes—an "ower"—would look like [ˈoʊ ɚ], shown in two syllables in the transcription. Just like on the other side of the vowel triangle, with the [ɪɚ] diphthong, keeping the primary vowel sound more open helps us go smoothly to the round-off vowel without breaking

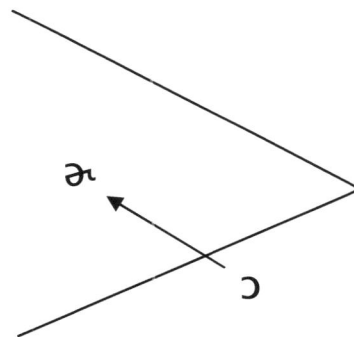

into two syllables. Keep in mind also that with the use of diacritics, we can actually show the [ɔ] sound as being a little more closed anyway by placing a small curved line underneath the symbol, like so:

horse   [hɔ̜ɚs]

But whether or not you use the diacritics, keep an open mind (and ear), experiment with the sounds of the [ɔɚ] diphthong, and learn to hear it and sing it in a more open way than perhaps you've been used to. There's no need to open it up too much though—remember, we already have an [ɑɚ] diphthong.

The [ɔɚ] diphthong is often, but not always, spelled /or/, as seen below:

or	[ɔɚ]	o'er	[ɔɚ]
core	[kɔɚ]	course	[kɔɚs]
pour	[pɔɚ]	forced	[fɔɚst]
fords	[fɔɚdz]	gorge	[gɔɚdʒ]

Note: The poetic word "o'er" is another contraction—for "over"—this time changing the sound of the open /o/.

Transcribe the following words, using the [ɔɚ] diphthong, into IPA:

adored	[ ]	boarding	[ ]
chores	[ ]	more	[ ]
restore	[ ]	ignores	[ ]

Now transcribe these words from IPA into their orthographic spelling:

[pɔɚt]   _____   [kɔɚts]   _____

[ɹɪ ˈstɔɚd] _____   [ɹɔɚd]   _____

[flɔɚd]   _____   [ˈspɔɚ tɪŋ] _____

As with the other previous diphthongs, in the context of singing a legato phrase, the sound of the hooked schwa may change to the hard /r/ consonant in linking into an oncoming vowel. Let's look at the word "for," which looks like [fɔɚ] in transcription. With the [ɔɚ] diphthong, the phrase "for ever" becomes [fɔ ˈɹɛ vɚ], (the same as "forever") with the /r/ in the word "for" getting less energy than a regular initial consonant, because it's linked and acting as a medial. (It's easier to see it as a medial consonant in the "forever" spelling.) Again, the diphthong is now missing from the word "for," as the /r/ sound is linked into the next syllable, depending on the tempo.

[ʊɚ]

The last of the hooked schwa diphthongs is the [ʊɚ]. As we have seen previously with the other diphthongs, again we sustain our [ʊ] position, rounding off to the hooked schwa at the end. Keeping the primary vowel sound more open (more open than a closed /u/ vowel) helps us in smoothly going to the round-off vowel without breaking into two syllables. For instance, the word "your" looks like this in the IPA: [jʊɚ], rather than with more closed [juɚ]. As with the [ɔɚ] above, if we sang [juɚ], it would break into two syllables, like the word "ewer" [ˈju ɚ]—a kind of pitcher. Singing [jʊɚ] helps us not only stay more open, but it keeps the monosyllabic nature of the word intact.

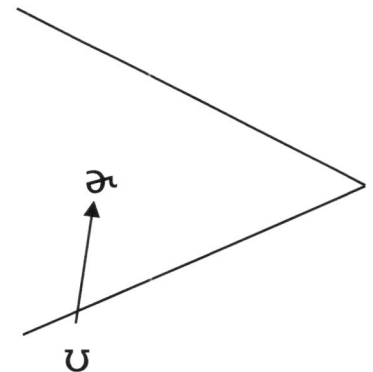

The [ʊɚ] diphthong is typically seen with /oo/ and /ou/ spellings, as seen in these examples:

poor   [pʊɚ]   boor   [bʊɚ]

Moor   [mʊɚ]   yours [jʊɚz]

Note: The last word uses a glide symbol for the /y/. Some diction texts list [ju] as yet another diphthong, but it's actually just a glide followed by a vowel. See the chapter on glides in the pages ahead.

Transcribe the following words, using the [ʊɚ] diphthong, into IPA:

sure   [   ]   lures   [   ]

velour [   ]   tour   [   ]

Note: The word "jury" doesn't use the [ʊɚ] diphthong, because the /u/ and the /r/ are in different syllables. It breaks as ['dʒʊ ɹi] in the IPA, and /ju-ry/ in English spellings.

Now transcribe these words from IPA into their orthographic spelling:

['ʃʊɚ li]   _____   [baɚd]   _____

[tɔɚn]   _____   [ʃɛɚ]   _____

[klɪɚz]   _____   [ə 'lʊɚ]   _____

Triphthongs: /ire/ and /our/	Chapter 7

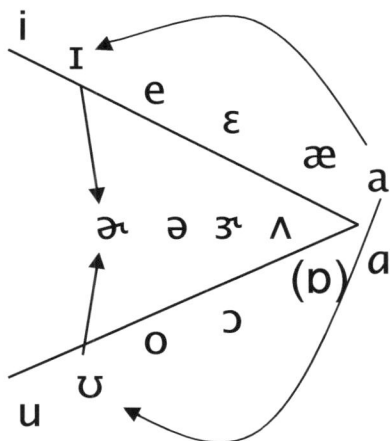

A triphthong consists of three vowel sounds adjacent to each other within a syllable. The two triphthongs in singing Standard American English are: [aɪɚ] and [aʊɚ]. As seen in the diagram to the left, both of them begin with the bright /ah/, then go through vowels on different sides of the triangle, and end up together again at the hooked schwa. Focus on making the transitions smoothly, with complete control of your articulators. Sing triphthongs as the monosyllabic combinations they are.

[aɪɚ]

In the [aɪɚ] triphthong, begin with the tip of the tongue—a relatively flat tongue—at the back of the lower front teeth, and with lots of space for a bright /ah/ sound, sustain it as the primary vowel. At the end of the note, briefly arch the tongue for the /ih/ sound while reducing the jaw space (the tip of the tongue is still at the back of the lower front teeth at this point). Then, with a slightly more open jaw space, the tip of the tongue quickly leaves the back of the lower front teeth and dips down, while the corners of the mouth pull in slightly. That's a lot of movement to control, but it can be done smoothly, and all on one note. Try singing the three vowel sounds in slow motion, treating the first one, [a], as the primary sustaining vowel, then ending with the [ɪɚ]. Gradually move through the sounds faster and faster, feeling the smooth transitions.

Here are some examples of the triphthong [aɪɚ] :

fire   [faɪɚ]   tire   [taɪɚ]

choir	[kwaɪɚ]	mire	[maɪɚ]
pyre	[paɪɚ]	expired	[ɛk spaɪɚd]

Some words we encounter in Standard American English sound as if they could be triphthongs, but actually break into two syllables, such as:

flyer [ˈflaɪ ɚ]	buyer [ˈbaɪ ɚ]	pliers [ˈplaɪ ɚz]

Can you hear and sing the difference between the following pairs of words? You might be more aware of the tongue arch in the two-syllable words, because the tongue transition is so smooth in the (monosyllabic) triphthongs.

Transcribe these words into IPA:

lyre	[ ]	liar (two sylls.) [ ]
dire	[ ]	dyer (two sylls.) [ ]

[aʊɚ]

Like the [aɪɚ] triphthong, the [aʊɚ] begins with the tip of the (relatively flat) tongue at the back of the lower front teeth. With lots of space for a bright /ah/ sound, sustain it as the primary vowel. At the end of the note, briefly arch the tongue in the back of the mouth for the "big /u/" sound while reducing the jaw space (the tip of the tongue pulls away from the back of the lower front teeth) and rounding the lips. Then, with slightly more open jaw space, the tongue quickly moves forward with the tip dipping down, while the corners of the mouth pull in slightly.

Again, that's a lot of movement to control, but it can be done smoothly. Remember from our study of the hooked schwa, we don't actually have to retroflex the tongue for the /r/ element within the triphthong.

Try singing the three vowel sounds in slow motion, treating the first one, [a], as the primary sustaining vowel, then ending with the [ʊɚ]. Gradually move through the sounds faster and faster, feeling the transitions smoothly.

Here are some examples of the [aʊɚ] triphthong:

our [aʊɚ]   hour [aʊɚ]   dour [daʊɚ]

Again, some words we Standard American English sound as if they could be triphthongs, but actually break into two syllables, such as:

shower [ˈʃaʊ ɚ]   coward [ˈkaʊ ɚd]   flower [ˈflaʊ ɚ]

But in their poetic form, some are seen contracted into triphthongs:

pow'r [paʊɚ]   tow'r [taʊɚ]   flow'r [flaʊɚ]

Transcribe these words into IPA—some of them two-syllable words, and others with a triphthong:

bow'r	[ ]	glower	[ ]
scoured	[ ]	frier (fry-er)	[ ]
inquire	[ ]	cower	[ ]
spiral	[ ]	tiring	[ ]

Note: In the last row of words, the syllable break means that the /r/ is used as a consonant following a diphthong.

Now sing these words/names and write the orthographic spelling for each:

[ˈkɹaɪ ɚ] _____   [ɪn ˈspaɪɚd] _____

[saʊɚ] _____   [ˈhaʊ ɚd] _____

| Glides (Semi-vowels) [j] and [w] | Chapter 8 |

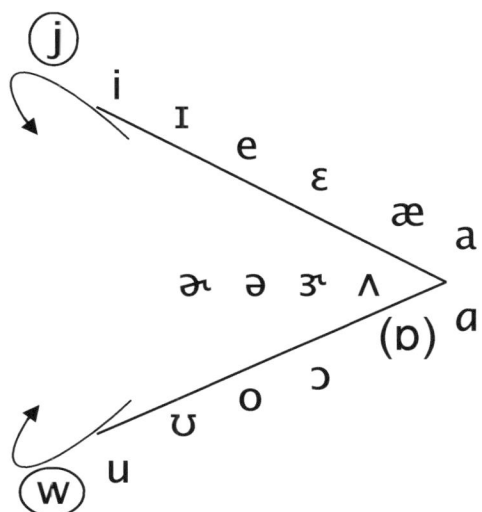

j

We will learn two other symbols used in the IPA of American English, the initial sounds in the words "yes" and "we."

Children learn that the vowels in English are: "a, e, i, o, u, and sometimes y." The "sometimes" part of the /y/ is that it can act differently—unlike the way a vowel normally would. Interestingly, in that sense, one could wonder about the "sometimes-ness" of the /o/ in the word "one" or the /u/ in the word "universe." These sounds act much like the /y/ in the word "yes" in that they are in a place between vowels and consonants called "glides." As you learn how these work, remember that they aren't only spelled with /y/ and /w/. Think about it—the word "union" actually contains the /y/ glide twice—neither spelled with a /y/. The IPA symbol is [j].

union   ['jun jən]

Take a look at the chart on the top left to see the position of the glides in comparison to nearby vowels. First, the [j] is related to the [i] vowel. For the [i], you'll recall, the tongue is arched up and forward, with the tip of the tongue lightly touching the back of the lower front teeth. If you were to sustain an /ee/ sound, then arch the tongue up and forward even more, then on to the syllable /ess/, you would go through the /y/ glide, ending up with the word "yes," kind of like "eeeeeee-**yes**."

We could say then that the [i] vowel is contained within the [j] glide. Visually, we could chart this as a progression like this:

i ⟶ j ⟶ ȷ

Another way to see the /i/ contained within the /j/ symbol is like this:

As we've seen, some of the spellings of the [j] glide contain a /y/, but there are many which do not.

Practice transcribing the following words containing the glide [j]:

yet	[	]	used	[	]
universe	[	]	you'd	[	]
confuse	[	]	beauty	[	]
opinion	[	]	pew	[	]
fusion	[	]	puny	[	]

Articles

One interesting thing that happens with an initial glide is that it makes a difference in the pronunciation of an article which precedes it. That is, we would sing "a" or "an" based on the vowel letter acting like a consonant in that sense. For example:

"an understudy"   but: "a union"   not: "an union"

Because the vowel letter is acting like a consonant (actually the [j] glide), the article changes as if it were a consonant also. The same is true for definite articles, just as for the indefinite ones above:

"the understudy"   [ði 'ʌn dɚ ˌstə di]

but: "the union"   [ðə 'jun jən]   not: [ði 'jun jən]

How does that make sense acoustically? The [i] and the [j] may be too close together to be easily heard as an actual change for the audience. Dropping to a schwa before the [j] then puts the sounds further apart for greater clarity. Think of the difficulty in singing the word "ye," for example. It could take an extra amount of jaw involvement to help the tongue make the articulation clear.

W

On the other side of the triangle, we have the [w], which, like the [j], is sometimes spelled with the letter we would normally associate with it, but not always. Here are a few examples:

won [wʌn]   one [wʌn]   was [wəz]   queen [kwin]

Note: the first two words are homonyms—that is, they sound the same; thus, the IPA is the same. Again, the accented or unaccented schwa could potentially be used, depending on the context within a song or aria, and how much stress is needed. The same is true for the third word, "was."

As we saw with the other glide (the [j]) in American English, [w] also has a vowel relationship. Look again at the vowel triangle and notice the proximity of the [w] to the [u]. As before, if you were to sustain an /ooh/ vowel, then slightly intensify it in terms of back-of-tongue arch, lip rounding, and jaw closure, you would end up in the position of the [w]. Try this: sustain the [u], intensify it through a [w], then open to the syllable [ʌn]. Sing the word "one" like this:

"oooooooh-**w**on"

We could say then that the [u] vowel is contained within the [w] glide. Again, we could chart this as a progression like this:

u ⟶ u ⟶ w

(morphing from /u/ to /w/)

Another way to see the [u] contained within the [w] glide is like this:

ω̈

Practice transcribing the following words, many containing the glide [w]:

wonder	[	]	wise	[	]
quack	[	]	guacamole	[	]
twins	[	]	quiz	[	]
switch	[	]	pew	[	]

Note: The last one is actually a trick question, since the /w/ in the orthographic spelling doesn't actually take a [w] in the IPA.

Glides are also known in diction as "semi-vowels." They can be thought of as part vowel/part consonant in much the same way a mezzo-soprano (literally "half soprano") is part soprano/part alto. They have a foot in each world and function seamlessly as sound-chameleons. (We baritones, of course, rather than feeling "part tenor/part bass," imagine that ours is the best and most important of the vocal ranges, and are therefore blissfully content in that self-satisfied perception.)

Some diction textbooks label the combination of /h/ and /w/ as a separate glide (/hw/ together), with its own IPA symbol, stating that the /hw/ is the unvoiced cognate of the voiced /w/. But if you slowly articulate the /hw/, you'll find that the /w/ glide is still voiced, coming right after the unvoiced aspirate /h/. As further proof, what do many people change [hw] to in their speech and singing? A [w]! Right—the [w] is still needing to be voiced, whether or not they remember to aspirate the /h/.

Another way to look at it is with an /h/ preceding the other glide—[j]. In a word like "huge," the IPA looks like this: [hjudʒ]. Wouldn't the /h/ be unvoiced and the [j] glide be voiced? Sure! It's the same way with the /h/ and /w/ in words like "which."

It can get tricky keeping up with when to use /hw/ versus /w/, /h/, etc. Here's a list of examples. The left-hand column contains words that do not use /hw/, but, instead, use just the /w/; the right-hand column has words which should be pronounced beginning with /hw/:

| witch | [wɪtʃ] | which | [hwɪtʃ] |

weather	[ˈwɛ ðɚ]	whether	[ˈhwɛ ðɚ]
(the letter) /y/	[waɪ]	why	[hwaɪ]
wear	[wɛɚ]	where	[hwɛɚ]
wipe	[waɪp]	whip	[hwɪp]
wise	[waɪz]	why's	[hwaɪz]
wine	[waɪn]	whine	[hwaɪn]
wide	[waɪd]	why'd	[hwaɪd]
wail	[weɪɫ]	whale	[hweɪɫ]
wile	[waɪɫ]	while	[hwaɪɫ]
world	[wɝɫd]	whirl	[hwɝɫ]
way	[weɪ]	whey	[hweɪ]
Will	[wɪl]	Wheaton	[ˈhwi tən]

Note: The last name can potentially be sung with the consovowel [ņ] in the second syllable, depending on the tempo of the song.

Remember that not all /wh/ spellings have the sound of [hw]:

who	[hu]	whom	[hum]
whose	[huz]	who's	[huz]
who'll	[huɫ]	who'd	[hud]
holy	[ˈhoʊ li]	whole	[hoʊɫ]

APPENDIX

TRANSCRIPTION PRACTICE 1

Practice transcribing these words into IPA. Remember to include the stress mark for multi-syllabic words.

1. hitch   [   ]   11. sandwich   [   ]

2. wheeze   [   ]   12. he's   [   ]

3. wipe   [   ]   13. white   [   ]

4. why'd   [   ]   14. wide   [   ]

5. we'd   [   ]   15. weed   [   ]

6. who'd   [   ]   16. wooed   [   ]

7. who's   [   ]   17. how   [   ]

8. thaw   [   ]   18. know   [   ]

9. whap   [   ]   19. whopping   [   ]

10. wince   [   ]   20. whence   [   ]

TRANSCRIPTION PRACTICE 2

Here's a little more transcription practice:

1. beauty   [   ]   7. booty   [   ]

2. cooped   [   ]   8. Cupid   [   ]

3. fool   [   ]   9. few   [   ]

4. who's   [   ]   10. Hugh's   [   ]

5. mood   [   ]   11. music   [   ]

6. confusion [   ]   12. contusion [   ]

Note the difference in the last line: in the first word, spelled with an /f/, there is a glide present, and in the second one, spelled with a /t/, ("contusion": an injury, such as a bruise) there is not.

TRANSCRIPTION PRACTICE 3

Now transcribe these words and phrases into their orthographic spelling and then sing them:

1.   [ju wɔnt wən waʃt] _____

2.   [ænd ðə 'wɪ nɚ ɹɪz] _____

3.   [juzd 'bʊk stɔɚ]   _____

4.   [seɪv ðə hweɪɫz]   _____

5.   [ə waɪld ɹaɪd ɔn ə ɹ'oʊ lɚ 'koʊ stɚ] _____

Note: In the IPA of the last line, if we think in terms of linking words in a legato manner, the words "on a" could look like this is the transcription: [ɔ nə], but since the /n/ is a linked final consonant, acting medially, and not an initial consonant (needing more energy), we can leave it at the end of the word "on."

102

TRANSCRIPTION PRACTICE 4

Here are more words for transcription practice with a wide variety of sounds:

1. idling   [   ]   19. infatuated   [   ]

2. whisper [   ]   20. leopard   [   ]

3. elephant [   ]   21. palatial   [   ]

4. figures   [   ]   22. esteemed   [   ]

5. poisoned [   ]   23. show'r'd   [   ]

6. inspiring [   ]   24. wooden   [   ]

7. confused [   ]   25. how's   [   ]

8. potion   [   ]   26. appalled   [   ]

9. toxic   [   ]   27. whisk   [   ]

10. tension   [   ]   28. wicks   [   ]

11. tuxedo   [   ]   29. tuxes   [   ]

12. artistic   [   ]   30. watch fob   [   ]

13. charred   [   ]   31. jeered   [   ]

14. impaired [   ]   32. afforded   [   ]

15. poorly   [   ]   33. Schirmer   [   ]

16. fluctuate [   ]   34. attention   [   ]

17. picture   [   ]   35. cucumber   [   ]

18. pitcher   [   ]   36. cummerbund [   ]

TRANSCRIPTION PRACTICE 5

Transcribe these words and phrases into their orthographic spelling:

1. ['æ lə ˌbæ stɚ] _____

2. ['kɹi mə ɹi] _____

3. ['aɪ zən ˌhaʊ ɚ] _____

4. [ɛg 'zɔɫ tɛd] _____

5. [ɹɪ 'fɹɪ dʒɚ ˌɹeɪ tɚ] _____

6. ['dɪk ʃə ˌnɛ ɹi] _____

7. ['tʃɛ ɹi ˌpɪ kɚ] _____

8. ['laɪ ənz ænd 'taɪ gɚz ænd bɛɚz oʊ maɪ]

   _____

9. ['sʌm hwɛɚ ɹ'oʊ vɚ ðə 'reɪn boʊ] _____
   (note the linked /r/)

104

TRANSCRIPTION PRACTICE 6

Now transcribe these phrases into IPA, keeping in mind any changes in pronunciation based on linking, sense stress, etc. Place the transcription above the words:

[   ]

1. He said you'd believe while in   Jericho, but   elsewhere....

[   ]

2. Think of this vision—shall we choose cookies   or   bucks?

[   ]

3. House boys burn fingers upon the old hay

[   ]

4. O divine Master, grant that I may not so much

[   ]

5. seek, consoled, understood,   loved, for in giving injuries...

[   ]

6. When we receive the budget, taxes

TONGUE TWISTERS

Here are a few tongue twisters for you. Enjoy articulating!

A Tree Toad

A tree toad loved a she-toad
Who lived up in a tree.
He was a two-toed tree toad
But a three-toed toad was she.

The two-toed tree toad tried to win
The three-toed she-toad's heart,
For the two-toed tree toad loved the ground
That the three-toed tree toad trod.

But the two-toed tree toad tried in vain.
He couldn't please her whim.
From her tree toad bower
With her three-toed power
The she-toad vetoed him.

Amidst the mists

Amidst the mists and coldest frosts,
with stoutest wrists and loudest boasts,
he thrusts his fists against the posts
and still insists he sees the ghosts.

A Tutor Who Tooted

A tutor who tooted the flute
Tried to tutor two tooters to toot.
Said the two to the tutor,
"Is it tougher to toot
Or to tutor two tooters to toot?"

ENDNOTES

[1]David Adams, *A Handbook of Diction for Singers: Italian, German, French*, second ed. (New York: Oxford University Press, 2008), xii.

[2]Geoffrey G. Foreward, with Elisabeth Howard, *American Diction for Singers: Standard American Diction for Singers and Speakers* (Van Nuys, CA: Alfred Publishing Co., Inc., 2000), 35.

[3]D. Ralph Appelman, *The Science of Vocal Pedagogy: Theory and Application* (Bloomington: Indiana University Press, 1967), 204.

[4]See the excellent questions teachers might ask themselves regarding their students in Victor Alexander Fields, *Foundations of the Singer's Art* (New York: The National Association of Teachers of Singing, 1984), 78-79.

[5]Virgil A. Anderson, *Training the Speaking Voice*, third ed. (New York: Oxford University Press, 1977), 130.

[6]Ibid., 130-141.

[7]Kurt Adler, *Phonetics and Diction in Singing* (Minneapolis: University of Minnesota Press, 1967), 5.

[8]James C. McKinney, *The Diagnosis and Correction of Vocal Faults: A Manual for Teachers of Singing and for Choir Directors*, rev. ed. (Nashville, TN: Genevox Music Group, 1994), 166.

[9]Kathryn LaBouff, *Singing and Communicating in English: A Singer's Guide to English Diction* (New York: Oxford University Press, Inc., 2008).

[10]P. Judson Newcombe, *Voice and Diction*, second ed. (Raleigh, NC: Contemporary Publishing Company, 1991), 12.

[11]Pierre Bernac, *The Interpretation of French Song* (New York: W. W. Norton & Company, Inc., 1976), 5-6.

[12]Martin Néron, "Coarticulation: Aspects and Effects on American English, German, and French Diction," *Journal of Singing*, Volume 67, No. 3 (January/February 2011), 313.

[13]http://ipa.typeit.org/ (accessed June 2012).

[14]Peter Roach, *English Phonetics and Phonology*, 4th ed. (New York: Cambridge University Press, 2010).

[15]Leslie De'Ath, "Linguistic Lingo and Lyric Diction II—Syllabification," *Journal of Singing*, Volume 67, No. 4 (March/April 2011), 427.

[16]Madeleine Marshall, *The Singer's Manual of English Diction* (New York: Schirmer Books, 1953), 14-15.

[17]Dorothy Uris, *To Sing in English: A Guide to Improved Diction* (New York: Boosey and Hawkes, 1971), 159-160.

[18]Joanne Harris Rodland, "At the Heart of the Matter," *The Chorister* 61, Number 1 (2009): 12.

[19]Amanda Johnston, *English and German Diction for Singers: A Comparative Approach* (Lanham, MD: The Scarecrow Press, Inc., 2011), 187.

[20]Uris, 68.

[21]Ibid., 22-30.

[22]See Rachel L. Lebon's discussion of "Microphone Singing Following Intensive Classical Singing" and "Classical Singing Following Intensive Microphone Singing" in her *The Versatile Vocalist: Singing Authentically in Contrasting Styles and Idioms* (Lanham, Maryland: The Scarecrow Press, Inc., 2006), 67-69.

[23]In order to better understand formants and their relationship to vowels, see the illustrations in Richard Alderson's *Complete Handbook of Voice Training* (West Nyack, NY: Parker Publishing Company, Inc., 1979), 124-125.

[24]Richard Miller, *The Structure of Singing: System and Art in Vocal Technique* (New York: Schirmer Books, A Division of Macmillan, Inc., 1986), 70.

[25]LaBouff, 266-272.

[26]Compare John Moriarty, *Diction: Italian, Latin, French, German...The Sounds and 81 Exercises for Singing Them*, seventh ed. (Boston: E.C. Schirmer Company, 1975), 20, to the vowel chart on the International Phonetic Association website, such as: http://www.langsci.ucl.ac.uk/ipa/vowels.html.

[27]See the interview with Luciano Pavarotti in Jerome Hines, *Great Singers on Great Singing*, fourth ed. (New York: Limelight Editions, 1988), 219.

[28]William Vennard, *Singing: the Mechanism and the Technic*, fifth ed. (New York: Carl Fischer, 1968), 142.

[29]http://dictionary.reference.com (accessed June 2012).

[30]John S. Kenyon and Thomas A. Knott: *A Pronouncing Dictionary of American English* (Springfield, Mass.: Merriam-Webster Inc., 1953).

[31]Vennard, 138-143.

[32]Uris, 159.

[33]Compare to Joan Wall, *International Phonetic Alphabet for Singers: A Manual for English and Foreign Language Diction* (Dallas: Pst...Inc., 1989), 100.

[34]Compare to Joan Wall, Robert Caldwell, Tracy Gavilanes, and Sheila Allen, *Diction for Singers: A Concise Reference for English, Italian, Latin, German, French and Spanish Pronunciation* (Dallas: Pst...Inc., 1990), 6.

[35]Joan Wall et al, *Diction for Singers*, 3.

BIBLIOGRAPHY

Adams, David. *A Handbook of Diction for Singers: Italian, German, French*, second ed. New York: Oxford University Press, 2008.

Adler, Kurt. *Phonetics and Diction in Singing*. Minneapolis: University of Minnesota Press, 1967.

Alderson, Richard. *Complete Handbook of Voice Training*. West Nyack, NY: Parker Publishing Company, Inc., 1979.

Anderson, Virgil A. *Training the Speaking Voice*, third ed. New York: Oxford University Press, 1977.

Appelman, D. Ralph. *The Science of Vocal Pedagogy: Theory and Application*. Bloomington: Indiana University Press, 1967.

Bernac, Pierre. *The Interpretation of French Song*. New York: W. W. Norton & Company, Inc., 1976.

De'Ath, Leslie. "Linguistic Lingo and Lyric Diction II—Syllabification." *Journal of Singing*, Volume 67, No. 4 (March/April 2011): 427-435.

Fields, Victor Alexander. *Foundations of the Singer's Art*. New York: The National Association of Teachers of Singing, 1984.

Foreward, Geoffrey G., with Elisabeth Howard. *American Diction for Singers: Standard American Diction for Singers and Speakers*. Van Nuys, CA: Alfred Publishing Co., Inc., 2000.

http://dictionary.reference.com (accessed June 2012).

http://ipa.typeit.org/ (accessed June 2012).

http://www.langsci.ucl.ac.uk/ipa/vowels.html (accessed June 2012).

Johnston, Amanda. *English and German Diction for Singers: A Comparative Approach*. Lanham, MD: The Scarecrow Press, Inc., 2011.

Kenyon, John S., and Thomas A. Knott. *A Pronouncing Dictionary of American English*. Springfield, Mass.: Merriam-Webster Inc., 1953.

LaBouff, Kathryn. *Singing and Communicating in English: A Singer's Guide to English Diction*. New York: Oxford University Press, Inc., 2008.

Lebon, Rachel L. *The Versatile Vocalist: Singing Authentically in Contrasting Styles and Idioms*. Lanham, Maryland: The Scarecrow Press, Inc., 2006.

Marshall, Madeline. *The Singer's Manual of English Diction*. New York: Schirmer Books, 1953.

McKinney, James C. *The Diagnosis and Correction of Vocal Faults: A Manual for Teachers of Singing and for Choir Directors*, rev. ed. Nashville, TN: Genevox Music Group, 1994.

Miller, Richard. *The Structure of Singing: System and Art in Vocal Technique.* New York: Schirmer Books, A Division of Macmillan, Inc., 1986.

Moriarty, John. *Diction: Italian, Latin, French, German...the Sounds and 81 Exercises for Singing Them*, seventh ed. Boston: E.C. Schirmer Company, 1975.

Néron, Martin. "Coarticulation: Aspects and Effects on American English, German, and French Diction." *Journal of Singing,* Volume 67, No. 3 (January/February 2011), 313-325.

Newcombe, P. Judson. *Voice and Diction*, second ed. Raleigh, NC: Contemporary Publishing Company, 1991.

Roach, Peter. *English Phonetics and Phonology*, fourth ed. New York: Cambridge University Press, 2010.

Rodland, Joanne Harris. "At the Heart of the Matter." *The Chorister* 61, Number 1 (2009), 11-15.

Uris, Dorothy. *To Sing in English: A Guide to Improved Diction.* New York: Boosey and Hawkes, 1971.

Vennard, William. *Singing: the Mechanism and the Technic*, fifth ed. New York: Carl Fischer, 1968.

Wall, Joan. *International Phonetic Alphabet for Singers: A Manual for English and Foreign Language Diction.* Dallas: Pst...Inc., 1989.

Wall, Joan, Robert Caldwell, Tracy Gavilanes, and Sheila Allen, *Diction for Singers: A Concise Reference for English, Italian, Latin, German, French and Spanish Pronunciation.* Dallas: Pst...Inc., 1990.

ABOUT THE AUTHOR

John Blizzard serves as professor of voice/artist-in-residence at Wingate University in Wingate, North Carolina, where he teaches voice, diction for singers, and voice pedagogy. He has sung in opera, oratorio, and recital performances throughout the South, Midwest, Southwest, and Brazil, and earned degrees from Southwestern Baptist Theological Seminary (Master of Music and Doctor of Musical Arts), Florida State University (Bachelor of Music, *cum laude*), and Pensacola Junior College (Associate of Arts).

A member of Pi Kappa Lambda, the national music honor society, Dr. Blizzard has served as governor of the Mid-Atlantic Region of the National Association of Teachers of Singing (NATS) and in several positions as an officer in the North Carolina Chapter. He has also held a variety of music and worship leadership positions in churches in North Carolina and Texas, and has served since 2003 as Minister of Music at St. Stephen United Methodist Church in Charlotte, NC. He has also directed the choir of Temple Beth El in Charlotte during the annual High Holy Days since 1991, and is a Life Member of the American Choral Directors Association (ACDA).

In addition to various prizes won in singing competitions, Dr. Blizzard has received numerous academic honors, scholarships, and awards, including the Academic Achievement Award from the School of Church Music at Southwestern Seminary, and the Senior Music Award from the School of Music at Florida State University. He was given a Wingate/DuPont Summer Research Grant in 2001 to study the topic: *From Speech to Song: Southern Regionalisms vs. Standard American Speech in the Contemporary Song Recital*—findings from which he presented for the Southern Division of ACDA. He was also granted a sabbatical from Wingate to write this textbook during the spring semester of 2011.

The son of two teachers of English, polyglot John Blizzard has a passion for language. "Dr. B.," as he is known to his students, has a keen ear for the sounds (and their variations) of American English. Reared in Florida, Tennessee, and Illinois, he took eighteen hours of diction courses as a student, and has continued to learn and teach the concepts presented in this volume over the past twenty-five years. Dr. Blizzard has led international study trips to Vienna, Berlin, Lisbon, Hong Kong, Rome, and the Caribbean. An avid cyclist, he also enjoys spending time with his four grandchildren.

Printed in Great Britain
by Amazon